Please Read This for Me

Please ReadThis for Me

HOW TO TELL THE MAN YOU LOVE THINGS YOU CAN'T PUT INTO WORDS

Neil Chesanow and
Gareth Lauren Esersky

Arbor House · William Morrow · New York

Library of Congress Cataloging-in-Publication Data

Chesanow, Neil.
    Please read this for me : how to tell the man you love things you
can't put into words / Neil Chesanow and Gareth Lauren Esersky.
        p.   cm.
    ISBN 1-55710-016-0
    1. Communication in marriage.   2. Interpersonal communication.
3. Intimacy (Psychology)   I. Esersky, Gareth Lauren.   II. Title.
HQ734.C54   1988   88-12095
646.7'8—dc19   CIP

Printed in the United States of America

First Edition

1 2 3 4 5 6 7 8 9 10

BOOK DESIGN BY LINEY LI

PREFACE

What You Are Holding in Your Hands Is a Whole New Type of Relationship Book

How do you convince your boyfriend or husband that just because he happens to be a man, your job, your feelings, and the things you know are no less important than his?

What do you say to your guy when he's habitually late and doesn't bother to phone, or when he eyes other women at parties, or when he doesn't know his drinking is out of control? How do you tell the man you love that he isn't satisfying you in bed, and what he can do to really turn you on?

A COMMUNICATIONS BREAKTHROUGH

When you have something very important but really tough to tell the man in your life, wouldn't it be great if you could just reach for a book that starts the conversation for you, that spares you from having to stammer through those awkward opening lines, a book that quickly but acceptably confronts the sore spots in your relationship, each one clearly captured in a few choice words on a page or less?

Rather than leave those difficult thoughts unsaid—because

they are too embarrassing, too muddled, or just too hard to put into a man's language—imagine being able to check a key to the contents, turn to the appropriate page, give an open book to the man you love, and ask, "Please read this for me."

"What is it?"

"Just read it, okay? Page seventy-three. It's only a few lines."

And without further ado, give him *Please Read This for Me*. Once the man you love has the book in his hands, a glance will do the job. Each page is an emotional telegram. Yes, it's short, but it delivers your message with quickness and clarity, with just the right impact and sense of urgency so he knows that you really do need to talk.

A BOOK THAT DOES THE DOING FOR YOU

It doesn't matter what problem you choose to confront. It may be about work, money, sex, marriage, family, friends, being scared or feeling blue. Once his eyes sweep the page, the man you love knows what's been welling up inside you, bursting to come out. It's not ESP but it's the next best thing. It's as if you're showing him a Polaroid snapshot of your heart.

HAVE THAT SIGNIFICANT DISCUSSION

Use *Please Read This for Me* to get even tough conversations off the ground. Use it to start talking about sensitive issues that aren't easy to put into words. Personal things you want to share with the man in your life. Feelings you'd articulate if only you could—and persuade him to listen!

Here's that little push of forward momentum you two may need. *Please Read This for Me* is more a *communication stimulant* than a book in the ordinary sense. Unlike the typical relationship book, it doesn't try to show you *how* to communicate. The book itself can *be* the communication. Find the right page, give it to your guy, and with the simple act of a book changing hands, you rid yourself of the Number One roadblock to real communication: just getting started.

142 FRESH STARTS

Please Read This for Me may be slim, but packed between these covers are 142 conversations already begun, each a springboard to launch you into a significant discussion. We call these conversation starters "articulations," for they give you an easy way to articulate to your man—just by showing him the appropriate page—all sorts of difficult, vague, embarrassing, elusive, troubling, confusing, or complex thoughts, plus many traditionally "between-women-only" thoughts that most men are not aware of.

AN IDEA WHOSE TIME HAS COME

Please Read This for Me is based on a surprisingly simple premise: *Anything* you can think about you can talk about with your man without guilt, fear, or shame. And if what's on your mind is really bugging you, it *has* to be talked about with your partner if the two of you are going to work things out.

So in this book you'll find articulations on just about everything: love, sex, intimacy, emotions of all kinds, relationships with all types of people, money, work, power, health (his and yours), things you love, things you hate—a whole galaxy of things you feel that are really quite common, normal, and perfectly okay, yet are still hard for most of us to just come right out and say.

Please Read This for Me doesn't claim that talking alone is an instant cure for every relationship problem. But it does suggest that non-threatening communication is the common-sense approach to problem solving. It also maintains that keeping silent is a guarantee that nothing will change.

MESSAGES FOR YOUR MAN AS WELL AS YOU

The articulations in *Please Read This for Me* turn thoughts into words, a woman's silence (or a man's) into a couple's conversation. Giving this book to your man is like putting a key into the ignition of a car and giving it a twist. The engine responds automatically, starting the communication process by which even long-standing problems can be overcome.

In a sense, then, *Please Read This for Me* is like a foreign-language interpreter. But instead of translating French into English, it translates your special sensibilities as a woman into feelings a man can comprehend, identify with, and respect the importance of.

Please Read This for Me speaks a man's language on a woman's behalf. But it doesn't just speak to the man you love woman-to-man. It speaks to him heart-to-heart.

How We Got the Idea

Two summers ago we were having lunch in a New York restaurant. The conversation turned to self-help books about relationships. Wouldn't it be great, we mused, if there were a book that went beyond how-to, a book that—instead of showing you *how* to broach sensitive subjects with your boyfriend or husband—did it for you?

We pushed our plates aside. We took out legal pads. We uncapped our pens. That's how *Please Read This for Me* began.

Who elected us the big experts on relationships?

Well, nobody.

But we did have a couple of things going for us.

For one, Neil's ten years of writing for the leading women's magazines gave him a unique perspective: that of a man in a woman's world. While researching and writing articles, he had interviewed nearly 2,500 women on all sorts of subjects, from sales to sex to self-esteem. Often his interviewees would say, "Hey, you're a guy, and it's easy to talk to you. How come it's so hard to talk to most men about money? or intimacy? or love?" Of course, there were no easy answers, but he began to wonder if there might not be some way to help women find answers for themselves.

Gareth's ten years of editing books for and about women sensitized her to just how hard it is for a book—*any* book—to offer a woman genuine help in talking uninhibitedly with a man, especially if the subject is delicate, especially if it's the man she loves. She had been thinking about the possibility of a new kind of book, one that would let a woman be more interactive, something she could really use to get those tough conversations off the ground.

In addition, our life experiences offered us plenty of raw material. Neil, though single, has had two long-term relationships, and there's a new, special woman in his life. Gareth dated her husband for three years before marrying him in 1985.

Does that make us perfect? Hardly. But we've put in some time.

In fact, when we try to talk with our significant others about something important, we probably have just about as much success—or lack of it—as anyone else. However, being an author and an editor, when speech fails—at least, at first—it's natural for each of us to grab a piece of paper and dash off a note

9

to our loved one that attempts to articulate more clearly what we were trying to say. And those little notes have worked well for us, serving as springboards for discussions that we might not otherwise have had.

And then, in a fortuitous moment over lunch, all these insights, thoughts and experiences suddenly jelled into *Please Read This for Me*.

SOMETHING TO SHARE

What we felt women really needed was a kind of tool in book form—a collection of little communiqués on a host of topics—to share with their partners. It was a need we could readily identify with. We had experienced it ourselves.

But which topics? The possibilities seemed limitless. We realized we needed to speak with a lot of women to see which relationship problems were the most universally shared. So we met with groups of working women in their offices and housewives in their homes and conducted formal interviews, asking prearranged questions, recording the conversations on tape, making transcriptions, and studying the results. But there were also plenty of informal gettogethers over coffee or tuna sandwiches that were just as valuable.

We wanted to speak with all kinds of women who did all kinds of things and lived in all kinds of places, so while many of our interviews were conducted face to face, many others were done over the phone. In fact, our phone bills started to go through the roof as we spoke with women from Maine to California and from Quebec to Vancouver.

LOTS OF INPUT

When the smoke finally cleared, we had talked with secretaries, managers, and business executives, nurses, doctors, lawyers, bankers, and dentists, insurance brokers, real estate agents, saleswomen of all kinds, teachers, artists, scientists, and engineers, new mothers, single mothers, grandmothers—you name it.

We interviewed a policewoman, a female jet pilot, a woman dog trainer, and a woman ski instructor. We spoke with women who are married, who are single, who are "living-withs," women who are divorced, widowed or engaged, women who are old, young, in-between. We talked with women in happy relationships, with women who are separating or considering it, with women who are reconciled to staying with the "wrong" man (by their own admission), those who are thinking about having kids, and those who feel they probably will have none—some by choice, but not all.

We remember the Detroit fireman's wife who feels anxious—and angry—when her husband, knowing he's going to be late from work, neglects to phone. And how could we forget the Philadelphia manufacturer who employs her husband, a role reversal that sometimes strains their relationship. Or the workaholic couple, both Wall Street stockbrokers, whose sex life suffers due to sheer fatigue. Or the wife who is the business traveler while her husband, a teacher, remains at home in Boston and frets—without cause, but nevertheless—about her fidelity. Or the young couple who went steady during their four years at the University of Houston and are now tasting the freedom of life after college, finding temptation tugging at their relationship.

These stories and many others helped to inform and enrich *Please Read This for Me*. In a society like ours, where just about every type of relationship is possible, you would expect the problems that couples experience to run the gamut, and they do—from lack of romance to lack of respect, from constant arguing to constant silence, from suffocating attention to sheer indifference—but after we sorted all of them out and grouped them into categories, now chapters in this book, what emerged as the number-one concern was *communication.* "I know what I mean to say," women told us repeatedly in many different ways, "but how can I get him to really understand?"

THE RESULT

Here, at last, is a place to start. Neil's girlfriend has used *Please Read This for Me* to get *him* to understand things that never quite sank in before. Gareth has used it to open up discussions with her husband. Many women volunteered to test the book on the men they loved. Of course, they had varying degrees of success, but most had definite success. It works!

"Oh, is *that* what you meant?" was a typical male response. And sometimes it *was* what she meant. But often that wasn't exactly it. But now at least she had a foundation on which to build. Having taken a step toward real communication, she could then refocus, and refocus *again* if necessary, until her man truly *did* understand.

That is the process *Please Read This for Me* is designed to begin.

ACKNOWLEDGMENTS

Some people deserve special mention for their generous support, good ideas, sage advice, and constructive criticism. Thank you all.

Sharon Almeida; Lori Ames; Cheryl Asherman; Geri Bain; Rochelle Balter; Meg Blackstone; Jonathan Blumenfeld; Lois Blumenfeld; Ethyl Blumenfeld; Leslie Breed; Wanita Burrell; Liza Dawson; Mildred Dawson; PJ and Dr. Michael Dempsey; Lisa and Jason Dolin; Pam Dorman; Suzanne Ekman; Rheta Esersky; Martha Esersky; Ellen Feinsand; Cathy Fox; Pattie and Barry Glynn; Susan Halligan; Alison M. Harrison; Faith Hornby; Werner and Debbie Jurgeleit; Susan Kohl Katz; Kathy Kiernan; Hilda Levitan; Rhoda F. Levin; Carol Mann; Barbara and Larry Marks: Sandra Medallis; Joan and Aric Mills; Carole Monroe; Barberi Paull; Ruth Pickholtz; Jane Rosenman; Lisa Queen; Bettina Rosser; Brenda Segel; Dagmar Stock; John Stuart; Stephanie von Hirschberg; Deborah Weiss; Leslie Wells.

WRITE TO US

If you have ideas for articulations that you believe to be common problems for women who are trying to relate to men—or even for men who are trying to relate to women—and you don't find them in these pages, we'd like to know what they are. Your thoughts may help a lot of people, and that's what *Please Read This for Me* strives to do. Please type or write neatly and mail your letters to: PLEASE READ THIS FOR ME, Arbor House/William Morrow and Company, Inc., Department GC, 105 Madison Avenue, New York, New York 10016.

Thank you.

CONTENTS

INTRODUCTION

Making the Most of
Please Read This for Me

You've probably already browsed through *Please Read This for Me* and seen how it can work. Still, the book is deceptively simple, so here are some notes to help you and the man you love use it more effectively.

Short Is Sweet

The articulations are short. Why? If you've ever tried to share a 300-page relationship book with a man, you know the answer. It's just too long—even if he really would like to know what's inside. Now the sheer length of the message won't be an obstacle—for you or for him.

No Hints

Because the articulations are untitled, one page looks just like another. A person actually has to *read the words* to see what a given message is about. That's the idea. If there were a title at the top of each page, like *Sex*—which is just as tough a subject for men to talk about as it is for women—your partner might hand the book back without reading Word One. The articulations are untitled to prevent this from happening.

The Key Is Your User's Guide

You, of course, need to know what articulations are in *Please Read This for Me* and where they are. In the Key, they are grouped into chapters by subject—*Sex, Emotions, People, Work,* and so on. The first sentence of each articulation expresses its theme and is listed there, in the same way that the first sentence of a poem may serve as its title.

For Faster Reference, Check the Index

With 142 first sentences, the Key is a little long. So at the back of the book, the Index is organized the same way—the articulations are grouped into chapters by subject—but instead of listing them by first sentences, the Index simply lists them by *subject.* For example:

KEY

41   II. LOVE AND INTIMACY
_____

42   Whatever happened to candlelight, candy, and flowers?

INDEX

Don't Expect Every Articulation to Have Your Name on It

Please Read This for Me covers lots of relationship problems women typically have with men. But many of them won't be *your* problems, thank goodness. If every articulation related to you, you'd probably qualify as the world's most unhappy person.

But some articulations are bound to hit home. And others, which may have no bearing on your relationship now, may express just what you feel next month or next year. So *Please Read This for Me* is really a book you can have and use for a lifetime, a book you can turn to and share again and again as you and the man you love continue to change and grow.

HOW TO USE *PLEASE READ THIS FOR ME*

You may want to hand *Please Read This for Me* to your guy and say, "Would you please read page forty-five for me? It'll only take a second and it would mean a lot to me." Or you may want to use the bookmark to identify the articulation you want him to read, and then leave *Please Read This for Me* for him to "discover" somewhere—on his pillow, for instance, or beside his morning coffee, or on the arm of his favorite chair—places where you know he'll be at predictable times and in a receptive frame of mind.

But use *Please Read This for Me* in the way that makes *you* feel most comfortable. If you'd rather not hand someone a whole book, you can photocopy the page that articulates your thoughts. Or, if an articulation comes close to expressing what you feel, but it isn't quite right, and you want to add something to it, go right ahead and put it on the page. Feel free to write your own note. Because each articulation contains only a few words, you can simply copy out and adapt the message onto your personal stationery, or a pretty note card, but just an ordinary sheet of paper is also fine.

The main thing is to use *Please Read This for Me* as a way to start *communicating* with the man you love—communicating in a way he can hear, maybe for the first time since the two of you met, feelings that mean so much to you but that he's never quite understood before.

The idea of *Please Read This for Me* is to get you two talking about issues that really matter to you both. Will that magically make everything right? No one can promise you that. But you'll be amazed at how many problems you thought had no solution that the normally not-so-simple act of clear communication will suddenly start to improve.

That's what *Please Read This for Me* helps you do: Get in there and start talking about what's not right in your relationship and how to go about fixing it.

5 TIPS FOR BEST RESULTS

1. Don't try to communicate when the man you love is tired or upset. No one likes to be confronted with a problem in these circumstances.

2. Even though some articulations express anger, wait until you feel ready to have a real conversation with your man—not just an argument—before showing him an angry articulation. Not many problems get worked out in the heat of anger.

3. You'll probably find more than one articulation that says, "Hey, this is me!" If so, don't try to get your guy to read a bunch of them at once. You'll only overwhelm him with too much on too many pages, exactly the opposite of what *Please Read This for Me* is intended to do. Pick *one* articulation, show it to your man, and save the rest for other times. After one articulation is used to launch your first significant discussion, you'll both find it easier to start using others.

4. After glancing at an articulation, if your man makes a sincere attempt to respond, it's a sign that you're on the

right track. But he may not respond right away. Some men do. Others take a little longer. This doesn't mean your man is immune to conversation. Give the message a chance to sink in.

5. A word of advice: If your guy is hooked on drugs or booze, or if he abuses you physically or sexually—anything *that* extreme—you need professional help. *Now.* Check the index of your Yellow Pages under "Counseling." Just pick a name you like and dial the number. Or ask a friend, a coworker, a family physician—*someone*—for a recommendation. Don't think about it. *Do* it.

KEY

44 You used to be a great kisser, but do you still have the stuff?

45 I hate it when you take me for granted.

46 The last time you told me you love me seems like 1888.

47 You say things that hurt me, and I don't even think you're aware of what you say.

48 How do I know you love me if you never show it?

49 I can stand right beside you and feel like we're a mile apart.

50 I love you but I don't know if I like you.

51 I love being part of a couple with you, but I still need my space, my time, my say.

52 I may let my guard down with you, but it's not an invitation to attack me.

53 Can you show me the man behind the mask?

54 I love surprises, but I don't want our relationship to be one of them.

55 III. COMMUNICATION

56 You have ways of talking to me that have nothing to do with what you're saying.

57 Why aren't you sharing your feelings with me?

58 We need to call a cease-fire.

59 I wish I could tell you what I tell the girls.

60 You're not a good enough actor to lie to me.

61 When you tell me the truth, do you always have to be so honest?

62 What can I do to get you to talk to me?

63 Just because I'm more sensitive than you doesn't mean I can read your mind.

64 How come we each speak English as if it's a different language?

65 Talk is cheap but communication costs.

66 IV. EMOTIONS

67 Why am I the target if it's not me you're angry at?

68 It's time to get serious about taking me seriously.

69   I can't always swallow my anger to suit you—or even me.

70   Everyone is entitled to be in a bad mood.

71   I wish I could always explain why I feel anxious.

72   When I have a panic attack I really need your help.

73   Do you know what my biggest fear is? Uncertainty.

74   I just looked in the mirror and you know what I saw? You dumping me.

75   Just because some guy touches my arm, it doesn't mean we're sleeping together—or want to.

76   Hey, tough guy, don't say, "Don't worry about me."

77   Women aren't the only ones who are moody.

78   Would you please not interrupt me when I'm talking?

79 V. GROWTH

80   I want you to nurture me the way only a man can.

81   I want us to have something to show for our relationship.

82   You act like Cary Grant in public and Archie Bunker at home.

83   Howdy, stranger.

84   When I imagined finding someone and falling in love, this wasn't exactly what I had in mind.

85   Let's reach out and touch someone: each other.

86   Are we still a couple or two ships passing in the night?

87   I always thought our love would grow. It seems to me that we've been stuck in the same place for a long time.

88   I need you to accept—and appreciate—that I'm not the same woman you first met.

89   I've decided to make an investment in myself.

90   When I see other couples split up, it scares me.

91   Why can't you just accept me for who I am?

92   I'm afraid if I do what I really want to do it'll push us apart.

93   I'm not a girl just like the girl who married dear old Dad.

94   I want to take more chances but I need you to stand by me.

24

119   I don't want our next vacation spoiled by things we feel obliged to do.

121   I don't know about you, but I need a *real* day off.

122   VIII. PEOPLE

123   Do your friends like me?

124   My friends can't believe that two people as different as we are can have a real relationship.

125   The people you work with seem cut from the same cloth: burlap.

126   The people at my job are starting to play guessing games about what you're like.

127   When I see you kiss another woman on the cheek, my heart skips a beat.

128   I wish you wouldn't treat my guy friends like the competition.

129   If your boss and you aren't related, why do I feel like he's a member of the family?

130   When we're socializing as a couple, you can turn from Dr. Jekyll into Mr. Hyde.

131   Guess who my favorite people aren't?

132   Being in love doesn't mean we have to tell our friends, "Sorry."

133   IX. FAMILY LIFE

134   I think about marriage all the time.

135   It could be I'm falling out of love.

136   You'd probably prefer it if I were an orphan.

137   Your parents make it clear I'm not the girl for you, and I'm still waiting for you to object.

138   It's hard to believe you and your brother have the same parents.

139   My sister and you may not see eye to eye, but I love you both.

140 Relating to your family can wear me out.

141 I know your mom has always come first, but now I want equal time.

142 We don't have to wait for a holiday to visit our folks.

143 Do we have to go home for the holidays every single year?

144 I need a vacation from family life.

145 We've talked *around* having a baby. Let's talk *about* it.

146 I don't need to have children to feel complete.

147 We can't have a child on our own. What are we going to do about it?

148 Maybe I'm not ready to have a baby.

149 X. WORK

150 Can we talk about something other than work?

151 I'm sorry you got fired, but it didn't happen yesterday.

152 I've always wanted my own business. I'm going for it.

153 You may have a demanding job, but you need to do more than just squeeze me in.

154 If you were offered a great job in another part of the country, would you ask me before you said yes?

155 Until I get settled at my new job, I'm probably going to be distracted, exhausted, and nervous.

156 The fact that I got promoted makes us both look good.

157 I guess this wasn't your year.

158 Just because you make more money than I do doesn't mean my job is less important than yours.

159 Do you think that just because I work at home I've got time to do all your errands?

160 I'm afraid people will find out who I really am: just a little nobody.

161 XI. MONEY

162 I hate doing the same job as men and getting paid less for it.

163 You say I spend too much. I say I don't.

164 Let's treat saving money like a habit, not a chore.

SEX

If the prospect of even peeking at an articulation in this chapter—let alone sharing one with your man—makes you want to cringe, you're not alone. Nothing is tougher to talk about than sex. Here is your chance to make it easy *enough*. These articulations won't make your feelings of vulnerability, sensitivity, and possibly embarrassment disappear. But they will ease you gently into many significant discussions you need or would like to have with your man. And they will give you food for thought. When you show your man an articulation in this chapter, keep in mind that sex is probably just as difficult a subject for him as it is for you.

I think the hardest discussion to have is sitting on opposite sides of the room with our clothes on and talking about sex.

We both have such fragile feelings, and there's so much potential for unintentionally saying a wrong or hurtful thing, that I dread the idea of bringing the subject up.

But then I think, "You love this man. That you tiptoe around this issue is a sign of that love. Otherwise, you wouldn't care about his feelings so much. Still, you should be able to discuss *anything* with him—even this, *especially* this—for it wouldn't be such a delicate subject if we loved each other less."

It may be hard for me to hear it the first time or two, but would you give me some honest feedback about what I do in bed that you really like, what I could do better, and what I haven't been doing that we might try? Because I want our lovemaking to be as exciting, as fulfilling for us as it can be.

May I do the same with you? I want you to know what really turns me on about our sex life, what I find so-so, what I could live without, and what I think it might be fun to try.

Let's make a date to discuss how we might make love. It should be a time when we're both dressed, fairly relaxed, and reasonably comfortable sharing our sexual feelings in conversation . . . so we can share them better in bed.

I can remember when we used to have sex at least once a week.

It seems like a very long time since we last made love. I'm starting to feel sexually frustrated. And I worry that you don't find me attractive anymore. Or that maybe you're having an affair. Or that maybe you've lost interest in sex because of something I've done, or didn't do, or some way you feel, or don't feel.

We need to talk about why we haven't been having sex in our relationship. I've got plenty of good, strong desires for love, intimacy, and passion in bed. I'm sure you do, too. And I figure that you must have some genuine reasons why we're not having sex. Maybe those reasons don't have anything to do with me. Maybe it's pressure from work or some other concern: your family, your health, getting older—oh, I don't know.

But that's the point: I just don't know, and I really want to know—very much. Would you try to tell me what's happening with us sexually from your point of view? Because if it's something concerning me, maybe I can do something about it. And if it has to do with something else, at least I can try to understand it and be supportive to you so that, eventually, we can become lovers again.

When we have sex, it's just slam, bam, thank you, ma'am.

I wish you could see how you "make love" to me. You seem to be following a set of instructions:

1. Remove clothes, get on bed, climb on top of her.
2. Insert Tab A into Slot B. Thrust until orgasm.
3. Flop off her and fall asleep.

Sometimes I feel less like we make love than like we *manufacture* it. Would you consider sex from my point of view?

- Having sex with me isn't a race. If you climax in three minutes instead of ten, you don't win a medal. I think the longer and slower our lovemaking is, the lovelier it is.

- Making love isn't just copulating. Would you kiss me, too? Would you whisper something sweet to me, like how much you love me or how wonderful I make you feel?

- I'm a person, not a machine. Would you be gentler with me when we're in bed? You're so gentle with your clothes on. Just because we get naked, it's no reason to stop.

- The physical part of sex doesn't end just because you have an orgasm. I'd like to have one, too, and it isn't always possible to have an orgasm before you or at the same time. Instead of simply stopping, could you ask me if I want to go on?

- Even after we've both had orgasms, sex isn't over. Lying side by side, being with each other, smelling each other, feeling the warmth of each other's bodies—all that is also part of making love. If you kissed me then, and whispered little endearments, that would be lovely, too.

The next time we make love, could we try it this way? You may be surprised at how nice—and new—sex can be.

You know it takes me longer than you to get ready for anything. That includes sex.

The whole process of lovemaking often happens too fast for me. We kiss each other in our special way that signals sex, and suddenly we're in the bedroom, unbuttoning our clothes.

Couldn't we slow things down? Could we sit on the living room sofa and kiss each other tenderly first? We used to do that once, you know. I loved the way you'd caress me with your big strong hands, so gently they seemed to radiate love, and I'd start to get so excited.

I could get that excited again—but I need that buildup. I feel like we often rush into sex. I'd like to ease into our lovemaking, as if having sex with you was to be savored and enjoyed slowly and made to last and last because it's so delicious. Which it is.

Even though I love our lovemaking, there are many different sexual moods I may be in. Some are frankly lustful, perfect for wriggling out of our clothes and getting naked right away.

But there are also other, less physical, more intimate and spiritual kinds of moods I feel. And then I just want you to stroke my hair, nuzzle my neck, and maybe fondle my breasts while I nibble your ear and brush my cheek against yours. Everything is slower, more relaxed, so unhurried . . . our lovemaking has a gentler, mellower, less frenzied but no less beautiful sort of passion.

If we slow down, maybe we can get into foreplay as much as we enjoy having sex itself.

Lovemaking stops when you have an orgasm.
True ☐   False ☐

If you answered "true," I need to give you a makeup quiz, because one of the nicest parts of lovemaking is *after* the physical part, when we could be lying there beside each other embracing in a dreamy kind of bliss, or gently caressing each other, and really just *being* there together for a little while.

But with us, even when sex is terrific, it's as if we stop being a couple when we uncouple. You either go straight to sleep or get out of bed, go into another room, and don't come back. And I'm left thinking, "Hey, where'd he go?"

The quiet time after sex can be so peaceful and beautiful and loving that sex sometimes seems to set the stage for it as a sort of prelude, rather than it being something optional and secondary that comes after the good part, like dessert following the main course. I *like* dessert! Sometimes it's *better* than the main course.

The next time we make love, would you stay with me afterward? Would you fight off sleep if necessary? Would you hold me for a few moments, and let yourself experience being with my being? That's part of lovemaking, too. Give it a chance, and you might even find it's a rather nice finish to sex.

Why do we always have sex at the same time, in the same place, in the same way?

We still use the same lovemaking routine that felt natural to us when we were in the first throes of infatuation, but now that we have some history behind us, it feels predictable to me. Doesn't it feel predictable to you? You know what I'm going to do. I know what you'll do. And it's only by imagining fantasy situations that sex has a sense of surprise.

Why fantasize about situations that are easy to act out and perfectly harmless and probably fun to try? Why can't we make love just before dinner, or just before breakfast, instead of always just before bed?

Or somewhere other than always *in* bed!

Let's take a bath together. Let's do it in your favorite chair. Let's do it out in the car! Let's do it someplace different for once. I think we need a change of scenery, don't you?

And what's stopping us from trying new things? We could switch around our usual positions. We could make love standing up. We could do it in front of a mirror. We could do it in a closet. We might even say sexy things to each other while having sex.

Would we be the first? Would we be breaking laws? We wouldn't, so let's experiment. I feel dumb pretending that all the possibilities are taboo, just because, for us, some are new.

I'd like you to give me oral sex.

I know I haven't made an issue of it before, but if you're gentle, I find oral sex one of the most exciting possibilities of lovemaking, especially when it's *you*—the man I care about so much—who's doing it to me.

Maybe it isn't your favorite thing, but knowing how turned on it makes me may make it more stimulating for you, too. There's a particular way I like it done. It's really very simple. The next time we make love, will you let me show it to you?

I want to turn you on in bed, but I just can't act like a porno star.

When we first began to make love, you knew what my sexual repertoire was. I knew yours. And we both felt our love life was pretty terrific.

Okay, time has passed. The bloom is off the rose, and you feel free enough now to want to try some of your sexual fantasies. I understand. But I need you to understand that some fantasies are exciting precisely because they *aren't* real. If we were to do some things you dream up, it would cause me physical pain or mental discomfort, and that would spoil the joy I feel when we make love.

It can be frustrating, I know. But I hope you care about me enough not to go out and find some woman who'll do those things—or threaten me with that. And while it may seem unfair, that's what having a good relationship is about: learning to make successful compromises so that you get *enough* of what you want, without insisting on what nobody gets: everything.

That doesn't mean I don't care if our lovemaking is unexciting for you. I care very much. And I want you to continue to be open with me about your sexual needs. I'll try to fulfill as many of them as I can—even some I may not be personally fond of—because I love you so very much.

But an exciting sex life isn't based solely on how many exotic things we try, is it? Isn't it also based on how deeply we care for each other when we make love? I think it is. I hope you agree. But do you?

36

I want us both to get tested for AIDS.

I love you. I do. But ever since this horrible disease hit the news, sex hasn't been the same for me. Not that I spent a lot of time thinking about it, but I guess I thought that if you or I ever had a sexual problem, it would be something else, something less severe.

But AIDS is different. And not knowing—just not being sure—terrifies me so much that even if we stopped having sex right now and stayed celibate for the rest of our lives, my fears still wouldn't go away without medical proof.

I've asked around. We're talking about a simple blood test. It won't take long. It won't cost that much. We'll have the results. Then we'll know.

I hope and pray we're both okay. But if I'm not, or you're not, or we're both not, we'll face the consequences together and stand by each other—out of love.

But I feel myself get tense each time we take off our clothes, protection or no protection, and I wonder when I get aches or a rash or wake up in a sweat or just feel run-down whether it's just my period or a cold coming on or the first sign of something far worse.

I can't go on living life not knowing if I've really got a life left to live or if there's a stopwatch with my name on it—or yours—ticking away. I just can't.

What if I told you you're going to be a father?

Are you stunned? Are you thinking, "Oh boy, this couldn't be a worse time to have an unplanned pregnancy"? Are you ready to accept the responsibilities of fatherhood *now*? And the sacrifices that go with it?

If not, you're lucky. Because I'm not pregnant. No thanks to you. Because *I* use birth control and you don't. And if you think I *should* have to use it—and not you—because my body gets pregnant and yours doesn't, I've got news for you.

Short of sterilization, there is *no* foolproof method of birth control. I'm tired of having to be the responsible one—alone. I'm fed up with having to risk my health, and inconvenience myself, and endure discomfort, with you not showing a shred of concern.

I know you don't like condoms. You say they reduce the pleasure of sex. You say they're uncomfortable and inconvenient to wear.

Well, I say, "Join the club."

I want you to become a full partner in our sex life. I can't stop using contraception. There's too much at stake. You can't afford *not* to use condoms. For the same reason.

Accept it. Acknowledge that it takes two people to make love, two people to make a baby, and two people to practice *real* birth control, not just the woman in a relationship.

The next time we have sex, wear a condom. Don't make a fuss. Just do it. For me. For yourself. Do it for us.

There's only one absolute way to protect ourselves against AIDS and only one safe alternative.

One way not to have to worry about AIDS is to stop having sex. Does that sound extreme? Well, that depends. Put yourself in the shoes of someone who has AIDS now, only imagine you've got a choice. You can live out the rest of your natural-born life—but without sex—or do what you want and let the disease run its course.

Even in the world of make-believe, only one choice is unthinkable, and it's definitely *not* life without sex.

Luckily, in the real world, we don't just have one choice. We have two: life without sex, or safe sex with condoms.

If you think there's any other choice, find someone else to have sex with. Because much as I enjoy making love with you, I don't plan to die young.

The next time we go to bed, we're going to use condoms. And I'm going to show you how little they interfere with lovemaking when two people care about each other as much as we do.

Just because we start using condoms, it doesn't mean condoms have to come between us.

If you think that because you didn't get an erection I think you're not a man, we need to talk.

Even "real men" don't get erections every now and then. You're human, not a machine. People can't always be perfect. No one expects it. I sure don't. I wouldn't want a robot for a lover. I want you, imperfections and all.

Frankly, I'm glad you're not perfect. I'm certainly not. And I'd hate being around a man whose very existence constantly reminded me of my flaws.

Truth to tell, when we have sex, I'm not always lubricated and aroused. I might not feel well. I might be distracted or worried. I just might not be in the mood to make love, even though I'm willing to accommodate you.

But I don't go around feeling awful afterward. I wish you wouldn't, either. These things happen. It's no big deal. You're a great lover. You don't have to keep proving that. If you think I think differently, I really wish you'd let me know.

II

LOVE AND INTIMACY

If you've ever tried to talk about love or intimacy before, you may have given up on ever trying again. Granted, it *is* hard to take those abstract ideas and talk about them to a man as if they were solid objects like cars or tennis racquets, which is what many men seem to relate to best. You'll find these articulations are a good compromise. They still don't make love or intimacy three-dimensional, but they give form and substance to elusive issues like lack of romance, the importance of hugging, and the revelation of secrets that even a man can appreciate and understand. Don't be surprised if you show one of these articulations to your man and he says, perhaps for the first time: "Oh, so *that's* what you meant."

Whatever happened to candlelight, candy, and flowers?

Remember those sweet romantic gestures you used to make when we were courting? There were times when you rang my doorbell with a small token of your feelings for me. There were special evenings when you had planned some small surprise.

Do you know what I loved about that? They were ways of telling me you were thinking of me when I wasn't around. You were showing that you knew I cared about certain things, and by caring about them, too, you were showing that you cared about me.

When you brought me candy or flowers, do you know what I think I loved most? The surprise. It was so sweet. And your gifts and little attentions were so spontaneous and unexpected. You seemed to have an inexhaustible ability to be a dear, sweet, precious, adorable man.

I was really touched. I was enormously flattered. It made life seem more than just a humdrum daily routine. You were showing me that I added something meaningful and worthwhile to your life and you wanted me to know it.

By communicating that to me, you made my life wonderful and you made me feel so special, deserving, and loved. Can't we try to recapture that feeling? Don't you think we'd both enjoy really romancing each other once again?

Say, how about a hug?

What do I mean by "How about a hug?" You know what I mean. Don't give me that look. Just get on over here, put your arms around my waist, put your hands on my back, and squeeze gently, but with feeling. You know: *that* sort of hug.

Not a *bear* hug.

And not a pat on the fanny.

And not a pinch on the cheek, either.

I want a real, bonafide, genuine, authentic, old-fashioned hug.

I'll tell you why. Just because I haven't seen you. Just because I've missed you. Aren't those reasons enough for a hug? Hugs and kisses are precious when you're in love. Nobody can ever have enough.

Come on. Be a sport. Be a pal. Be a lover. Be a little romantic. You've got an extra hug or two to spare. We both know it. Out with them. Spread the wealth.

Maybe you'll get lucky and I'll give you a hug back.

With interest.

43

You used to be a great kisser, but do you still have the stuff?

Your lips used to set me on fire. A single smooch from you would triple my emotional electric bill for a month. When you gave me mouth-to-mouth, you could have brought me back from the dead.

Now if I get a peck on the cheek as you barrel out the door, it's a big deal.

When you give me a kiss when you come home from work, I'd like to time it with a stopwatch. But I can't. I couldn't turn the thing on and off that fast.

When you kiss me good night before hitting the sack, from the feel of your lips, you're already asleep.

Do you call that kissing? I've seen you dab your lips with a napkin with more attention and feeling than that.

I don't know. Maybe you're just past it. Used up. Kissed out. Numb-lipped. Over the hill when it comes to kissing. Yes?

If not, if you've got just one iota of kissability left in you, you'd better prove it to me—and quick!

Otherwise, I'll be forced to do something drastic, like ambush you in the kitchen, shove you up against the fridge, plant my lips on yours, and keep them there until my shoes start to smoke or your face turns blue, whichever comes first.

Consider yourself warned.

Kissing season is now declared open.

And you're fair game.

I hate it when you take me for granted.

You assume that when you come home from work, I'll be there to do things for you. You seem to think it's my role in life to be wherever you want me to be, to do whatever menial thing you need done.

Wrong.

You take for granted that I'll agree with whatever you say, that whatever decision you make on *our* behalf is automatically fine with me, that I'm your "Silent Woman."

The silence is over!

When you sign us up for a whole season's worth of football tickets without consulting me—committing me financially to attend every home game—it really makes me mad. I do want to be included in some things you like, but will you stop assuming that just because a given activity appeals to you it will appeal to me, too? I'm not your Siamese twin. Ask me, okay?

Must we have pizza with our best friends every Friday night? Once in a while, fine, but if you insist on locking it in as a weekly tradition, sometimes you'll just have to count me out.

Can we talk about some other things you take for granted I'll do, or be, or enjoy? You may find I've changed some—grown!— since the last time you bothered to ask.

When you meet someone new, you don't go making assumptions about that person. You can't. You don't know them well enough. I'm saying that as well as you think you know me, you don't know *everything*. Can you acknowledge that? Can you respect it? You don't know me inside out. You'll always be learning new things about me—if you just care enough to look.

The last time you told me you love me seems like 1888.

Can you honestly remember the last time you looked into my eyes and sincerely said "I love you" to me?

Can you recall the month?

How about the season? Last spring? Two winters ago? Three summers?

What about the year?

See?

It means more to me than you're apparently aware to hear you say those three little words. You used to tell me you loved me quite often, quite naturally, once upon a time. You once whispered it in my ear two, three, even four times a day!

Just because we've evolved from the pure simple lust of infatuation into the less torrid but richer and more complex climes of real love, that doesn't mean you should stop whispering little endearments. I need to hear them now more than ever.

And what could be easier? It just takes a moment. It's free. And it makes me feel wonderful. When you go out of your way to make me feel special, I'll go out of my way to reciprocate. You really get a lot of mileage out of three little words.

So say them to me once in a while.

What do you say?

You say things that hurt me, and I don't even think you're aware of what you say.

When I get a new haircut and ask how you like it, and you say, "Ah, you look like a dork" or, "Ugh, you look like a dyke" or, "That's the worst haircut you ever got"—I could just die. You make it seem like you couldn't care less about my appearance, let alone my feelings.

When I buy a new dress that I think makes me look pretty nice, so I model it for you, and you say, "You look fat"—it's as if you slapped me across the face. I want to burst into tears.

The thoughtless, negative, tasteless things you tell me destroy my sense of self-esteem. Don't you *know* that? You should. I'm tired of this verbal abuse. You're not a cruel person deep down— at least you didn't use to be—but when you make careless, nasty remarks, you seem like a real creep.

Would you please rehearse in your mind what you want to tell me, instead of just blurting it out? When you feel the urge to lash out, like a boxer jabbing with his right, for no reason other than to inflict pain, would you pause, catch yourself, recognize what you're about to do, reconsider, and then speak?

If you became more aware of how you predictably hurt me with your words, maybe you wouldn't be so quick to shoot from the hip.

How do I know you love me if you never show it?

You used to show me how much you cared for me in little ways. You'd take my hand when we crossed the street. I'm not a child. I don't need you—literally—to walk me across a street. But the touch of your hand and the concern it expressed made me feel that you truly loved me, precisely because it was such a small, sweet, sensitive thing to do.

Once, you phoned me when you knew you'd be late from work so I wouldn't worry. Or you'd call me at my job when it was raining outside to warn me to be extra-careful driving home.

And even though I might not have said a thing, you had a way of sensing the slightest change in my moods, and you'd ask me—unprompted—if everything was okay.

All that helped to give me the sense that you were taking care of me, and even though I'm a responsible, adult, independent woman, it was kind of nice. I felt like we were *more* than just lovers. I felt like we were really *in* love.

What happened to those small attentions? They've stopped. And I can't help but wonder, "Does he still care?" I miss the feel of your fingertips in the small of my back as you guide me into a room, and the touch of your hand on my arm as a show of sympathy or concern, and the way you once brushed my cheek with your hand—little things you once did so naturally to anticipate and see to my needs.

I miss them. Why have you stopped?

48

I can stand right beside you and feel like we're a mile apart.

You may not realize it, but sometimes you withdraw from me emotionally. I can sense it. You hide someplace deep inside yourself where I can't follow. It makes me feel like you're retreating into a bunker for protection against an aerial attack—and somehow, in a way I don't understand, *I'm* the enemy.

When you're in one of your states of "Red Alert," it doesn't matter if we're sitting on the same sofa in the living room or sitting on opposite sides of the same restaurant table or attending the same cocktail party, it feels to me like you're a thousand miles away.

But when I tell you that, you deny it. "What do you mean?" you say. "I'm right here." And physically, you are. But I think you are somehow afraid of getting too close to me, revealing too much to me, making yourself too vulnerable, because you're scared to death of being rejected—and maybe you've been rejected by other women before.

I promise I won't be one of them.

What I want more than anything else in the world is to have a *real* relationship with you. But that means more than just sharing physical closeness. It means sharing that side of you that you don't dare expose to anyone else, because it's been hurt before and the wound still hasn't healed.

I have wounds like that, too. Emotional bruises that are so painful to me I've been afraid to show them to you. But if we're ever going to close the gap between us, somebody has to make the first move. Or we could make a pact to do it together.

What do you say? I'll show you mine if you show me yours.

49

I love you but I don't know if I like you.

I know that you think if I "love" you, I *must* automatically "like" you, by definition—as if liking someone were just one small stepping stone on the road to love. Not true.

Liking someone isn't a lesser form of loving that person. It's a whole different thing—and no less important. The first time I laid eyes on you, presto: I was head over heels in love. You were the most fantastic thing in pants I ever saw. And it wasn't just your looks. It was your whole persona. Wow! Hot!

But like? Whoa, hold on there, Charlie. I didn't have the faintest idea if I liked you or not. We'd barely said a word—then. I hardly knew a thing about you—at the time.

Well, I'm starting to learn. And I have to tell you, when it comes to "like," the jury is still out.

Don't get me wrong. Sex is great. When it comes to passion— oh, brother, you really turn me on. And good looking? I couldn't ask for more.

But in other areas, I could. I am!

You ignore me. I don't like it.

You keep your feelings secret. It drives me nuts.

You get self-involved and forget that I exist. When you do that, I want to whop you one with a baseball bat.

I know some guys act that way. But those are guys I could definitely live without. Me? Like someone like that? No way.

So yes, you're terrific in bed, but do you have what it takes to be a pal? You've proved you have what it takes to be a lady's man. But can you handle the needs of a real woman? Because if you want me to *like* you, that's part of the deal. I want more than a lover. I also want a friend.

I love being part of a couple with you, but I still need my space, my time, my say.

This relationship is suffocating me. You have so many needs that require my attention that *my* needs too often get put on hold. Now it's time that I claimed some time for myself, and for the sake of our relationship, I need that to be okay for you.

So if I go off and do something on my own, don't give me the third degree. Don't poke and pick and probe and pry. I need some private time every now and then that's completely my own, and because it *is* mine, I don't want to have to feel obliged to give you a report.

This isn't the army. You're my friend. You're my lover. But you're not my commanding officer. When I go off on my own, I'm not going A.W.O.L. I don't owe you an explanation. Stop insisting that I do.

Look on the bright side. If you loosen up a little and give me more freedom to keep being me, when I'm with you I can *really* be with you, instead of part of me feeling resentful, neglected, and in the midst of an identity crisis.

If you give up a little of our time together, you'll get a lot more in return.

I may let my guard down with you, but it's not an invitation to attack me.

When I tell you about my fears, weaknesses, or worries, I need you to just listen and understand what I'm trying to communicate, because I'm stripping myself bare in front of you, and if you think it's easy or pleasant, believe me, it's neither. It's hard. It's frustrating. It can be scary, too.

And yet, when I feel *that* vulnerable, that's often when you clobber me with this macho attitude. Do this! Do That! Be practical! Curt suggestions. Harsh criticisms. Unwanted advice.

I'm not saying your advice isn't good—when it's asked for. But sometimes you shove it down my throat when I feel naked and exposed, and it's painful to hear then. It's as if you're dumping a pail of ice water on my head. It isn't appropriate. What I need is your love, sympathy and compassion, not cold logic.

When you throw a rock through my window like that and shatter the glass, you make me afraid to *ever* open up to you. I don't want to become like a hand-shy dog that cowers when someone tries to pet her because she's been smacked so often she doesn't know what to expect anymore.

Cut it out! Have a heart, will you? Not everything I reveal to you requires an expert, masculine, know-it-all response. Most times I just need you to be my audience for a moment. I'm *your* audience often enough. There's nothing wrong with my command of English. If I want your advice, I'll ask you flat out, "What's your advice?" Okay?

Can you show me the man behind the mask?

You've created this image of yourself that you're trying your hardest to fit, but it hangs on you like a badly tailored suit. The lines aren't clean. There are wrinkles in the wrong places. It's never going to look right because it isn't the real you.

I suspect—deep down I *know*—that underneath your carefully built facade is a pretty nice guy, someone I'd still like as a person and could love even more as a lover if he gave me half a chance.

But who exactly is he? Beats me. From the way you behave, you'd think there were a monster inside you, a little Godzilla clawing to come out. Do you know what's probably truly underneath all that armor? It's not some horrible beast. It's a nice, sweet, ordinary guy who's trying too hard to fit some super-hero mold.

Accept the fact that you're human like the rest of us, will you? Isn't it time to let go of the image and get in touch with who you honestly are? Remove the mask. You can be yourself with me. I'd much rather have the true you with all the imperfections than continue with this pretense. It's a no-win situation for both of us.

So come on. Get to like who you really are and let me get to like him, too.

I love surprises, but I don't want our relationship to be one of them.

You're like the original "Man of Mystery." Every time I think I've got you figured out, you give the plot a new twist. Trying to guess what you're going to do next is like trying to guess the murderer in an Agatha Christie story in Chapter One.

Will you quit your job to become a writer for a fortune-cookie company?

Or invest every dime of our savings in Himalayan real estate?

Or bring home a pet monkey or some weird bird or an icky snake that's ten feet long?

Life with you is a thrill a minute. I don't know if you'll build a raft and float down the Amazon or join a company based in Tasmania or wander out the door to get some ice cream and disappear off the face of the earth.

You think, "Hah hah"? Don't you hah-hah me. I'm trying to make a point!

I feel like I'm acting in an Alfred Hitchcock movie that doesn't have a script. I'm trying to have this sincere relationship with a guy I'm supposed to know, and then you throw me a curve ball by doing something totally out of character, and it's as if I never knew you at all.

Enough! I don't want the story of my life to be titled "The Woman Who Knew Too Little."

III

COMMUNICATION

Talking and communicating may seem the same. Not so. That's why so little *real* communication takes place in a couple. Often the woman tries to communicate by talking—but she's not being clear. And her man only makes it harder for her to express what she feels by paying half-hearted attention—or no attention at all. If this sounds like your situation, here is a set of articulations you can use. Make no mistake. Communication is still going to be tough. But these articulations will make it easier for you to get your man to hear and sincerely respond to issues you feel the need to address, from one extreme of communication—telling lies—to the other—feeling free to speak your mind.

You have ways of talking to me that have nothing to do with what you're saying.

I can tell when you're lying.

I can tell when you're nervous and upset.

I can tell when you're scared.

I can tell when you're uncomfortable with the people around you.

I can tell when you're enjoying yourself.

How do I know these things? All I have to do is look at your body postures or your facial expressions. When you turn away from me as you answer a question I ask you, I know you're not telling me the truth.

When you cross your arms and legs and you tell me you're not tense, I know better. The way you carry yourself, the way you hold yourself—they're clues to how you really feel.

But these are my interpretations. What if I'm wrong? Having to determine how you feel by reading your body language is defeating to both of us.

Sure, I can pick up the Morse code of your feelings even though you don't realize it—because I'm familiar with you. But I don't like to be left to my own devices to figure out the ways you feel. There are more easier, more effective ways to send these messages

Why aren't you sharing your feelings with me?

I make an honest effort to share my feelings with you. But you don't reciprocate. And I know that sometimes you feel hurt that I don't respond to some emotion or conflict going on inside you, when you haven't really taken the time to try to explain to me what the trouble is.

It's not that I don't care about your feelings. I do. I care about them very much. But often you don't give me a chance to offer the kind of sympathy I sense you want and need, not out of any lack of desire on my part, but simply out of lack of information.

I know that some men are brought up not to talk about their problems, and think that it's somehow unmanly to "burden" a woman with them. Well, I think that's wrong. I want to be burdened with what's bothering you because I love you, and sharing your burdens is one way I can express how much you mean to me.

Will you give me that chance? I know you don't want to trouble me, but you don't know how much it upsets me to see you suffering and not be able to help. It troubles me more to see you so closed up and so alone with your problems.

I have an idea. Why don't we sit down for just ten minutes each evening and talk about some specific feelings? Work. Relatives. Friends. Anger. Jealousy. And happiness, too—what makes us happy, what doesn't, what would. I can tell you one thing that would make me happy: the chance to be more of a genuine partner in your emotional life.

We need to call a cease-fire.

All we do is scream at each other. There's always something to fight about. Pick-pick-pick. That's all we do. Nobody wants to compromise. Neither of us wants to budge an inch.

We argue when one of us does something to threaten the other. Then the argument escalates because we each have an arsenal of weapons to attack with, amassed from previous fights. We don't argue because we disagree. We argue because you or I or both of us feel our self-esteem has been damaged and we want to inflict damage back.

I'm getting confused. What are we arguing about, anyway? Is the root of it a difference of opinion, or a breakdown in communication, or has something else gotten us upset, something that really has nothing to do with the battle at hand but is leftover wounds from some other war? Are we arguing about an issue or a reaction to an issue? You see what I mean? It's like we need a campaign map to figure out where we are.

Whatever happened to negotiating? All this arguing is getting us nowhere. It doesn't matter who's right anymore. It doesn't matter who started it. I feel like we're arguing for argument's sake. That's crazy.

I say we de-escalate. Let's call a disarmament conference, or at least diffuse the intensity of our attacks. If we just stop being so fiercely combative all the time, we can stop fighting and make a peace treaty, okay? It's the only sensible thing. Because all we're doing now is hurting each other, hurting our relationship, and hurting ourselves.

I wish I could tell you what I tell the girls.

There's a kind of intimacy I can easily reach by shooting the breeze with the girls. I suppose men can achieve something similar when talking among themselves. But hard as I try, I can't seem to get that same depth of understanding with the most important person in my life: you.

I somehow feel inhibited. I don't feel genuinely free to speak my mind, to tell you whatever enters my head. Instead, I strain things through a sort of filter before articulating them to you, and in the process something of the real me gets lost.

For instance, consider gossip. Women love to share details about other people's lives that rarely mean anything and are usually not true, but still, it's fun. I get a kick out of it. It comes as second nature to me. But because men tend to be critical of it, I stop myself from gossiping with you.

And yet gossip—dumb as it is—could be a common ground for us: something we could do together and laugh about. It could be part of the sharing process that frees us to reveal bits of ourselves that we might not feel safe to reveal at other times.

It's not that I want us to gossip. I want us to *share*. I wish we could just find a way to communicate with each other honestly and openly in a way that would make things between us feel less—well, pressured.

So I'm asking you straight out for once: Is it okay for me to be less inhibited with you in telling you some of the small, seemingly inconsequential things that go into conversation without having you say, "Ah, talk to the girls about that"?

You're not a good enough actor to lie to me.

You think it's easy to manipulate the truth to suit your purposes. It's not that easy. Sure, you can get away with it once in a while. But *which* times are impossible to predict.

And do you know why? Because I have a built-in lie detector. Five senses—no six—that automatically process every word you say, how you say it, your tone of voice, your facial expression, how you hold your hands—everything. I don't know if it's a blessing or a curse. Sometimes I wish it weren't so easy to tell when you're lying. Believe me, it hurts.

Worse, when you try to slip another lie by, my subconscious mental scorecard gets another entry, and collectively those entries subvert the feeling of trust I want to have in you. Then, when you tell me something implausible that *is* the truth, how can I believe you? My suspicions and past experience will keep reminding me, whispering "Once a liar, always a liar."

I don't want that to happen, and I don't think you do, either. So if I do something that discourages you from being straight with me, let's talk about it. I can't promise to react to every upsetting thing you do with poise, aplomb, and nonchalance, but I think we can reach some meeting of the minds. We'd better. Because I want you to be honest with me *all* the time, not just when there's no other way out.

When you tell me the truth, do you always have to be so honest?

I'm not just criticizing you for lack of tact, but there's being truthful and being Truthful with a capital *T*. When you use the truth as a weapon to justify hurting me because of some anger you feel, don't kid yourself. When you say, "Gee, I'm only telling you the truth; that's what you want, isn't it?"—the truth is beside the point. Hurting me—venting your anger at my expense—is the point.

When you criticize how I rush things, or how slowly I move, or how haphazard I seem to you, or how scatterbrained, or how fat—or whatever the weapon of the week happens to be—the last thing on your mind is being honest. You're out to search and destroy

And most of the time you succeed.

Now I'm asking you to try for a different, more difficult, but more rewarding kind of success. Yes, tell me the truth. I want that. I do. But please, do it out of love, not out of hate.

What can I do to get you to talk to me?

Bring in a marching band?

Swing from the chandelier stark naked?

Send you to a monastery where you can't talk to anyone for a month and make sure I'm the first non-monk you meet?

I thought I wanted a man who was the strong, silent type, but this is ridiculous. I've had it with the mummy routine. You're not dead, bandaged, and five thousand years old. You've got a mouth with a tongue that presumably works.

I think.

Prove it! Talk to me! I feel like I've been sentenced to solitary confinement. I'm dying of lack of conversation in this relationship. Somewhere inside those clothes you wear is a living, breathing, *talking* human being, and if memory serves—I'm straining here but I seem to dimly recall—he once had an interesting thing or two to say.

Yes? No? Don't just grunt. Don't just nod. Don't just shrug. And for Pete's sake, don't just go on being quiet!

Speak!

Just because I'm more sensitive than you are doesn't mean I can read your mind.

You sit there like a statue and expect me to somehow magically divine your thoughts, and then you get angry or frustrated when I can't.

Hey, I don't expect that from you.

In fact, when I tell you how I feel, half the time you get mad at me for trying to communicate my emotions to you.

Well, now I'm starting to get upset.

A lot of times you start to talk to me and before I've figured out what the real issue is that you're trying to articulate, you suddenly stop and say, "You know what I mean."

But I *don't* know what you mean! You have to tell me. That's what communicating is all about.

Please let go of your unrealistic expectations about the way you think I should respond to things I don't even know are going on. If you really want me to be responsive to your problems and tune into the same wavelength you're on, you've got to let me know what's really on your mind.

You know what I mean?

How come we each speak English as if it's a different language?

How can we approach the same subjects from two completely different points of view, as if you're from Venus and I'm from Mars, just because you're a man and I'm a woman? We might as well be speaking Chinese and Arabic. I don't understand you. You can't seem to comprehend a word I say. And neither of us can figure out how the other can fail to see things identically, when they're obvious.

I see mouthwatering escargots. You say, "Yuck! Snails!"

I see majestic Alps. You say, "Yeah, nice. Seen one mountain, you've seen them all."

I see suave, elegant, Italian design. To you it's foreign and weird.

Oddly enough, we may both be saying the same things. Tomayto, tomahto—in that sense. What I'm asking you, though, is to not dismiss or invalidate my point of view just because it's different from yours. Sometimes women have a different perspective on things from men. And part of it may have to do with me as an individual.

But "different" doesn't mean "worse"—or, for that matter, "better." Would you please just accept that my consciousness, while it may sometimes be different from yours, is equally valid and valuable? If we could just agree to respect each other's way of looking at life, it may help us both to see everything more clearly.

Talk is cheap but communication costs.

Simple talking and genuine communication are not the same. When you're trying to say something to me, and I don't get it, it doesn't mean you're not speaking clearly. And just because I don't understand, it doesn't mean I'm an idiot.

It means we aren't communicating. We need to try harder, that's all.

I wish you wouldn't get so frustrated when you fail to put your thoughts into words I can understand on the first try. I'll keep listening. Try again. Paraphrase. I'll get it.

And when I try to get a point across to you, and it seems like gibberish at first, you promptly lose interest. You tune out as if what I'm struggling to say couldn't possibly be valuable because it doesn't spring out of my mouth full-blown in perfect prose like the Declaration of Independence.

Hey, people don't communicate that way. We speak in sentence fragments. We grope for the right words. Our thoughts get all mixed up. But somewhere in all that seemingly shapeless blur of talk is a message fighting for life.

It takes two to communicate. Would you just hang in there? Would you ask an occasional question if you need more information? Would you make an honest effort to understand me? I'll do the same for you. I admit, it's hard. It's work. But if we keep at it, it's a skill we can use to share even complicated ideas with each other. Isn't that *true* communication? And isn't that what counts? The rest is just talk.

IV

EMOTIONS

What are emotions? They're your feelings, and feelings are awkward and clumsy to put into words. You know what you want to say, and yet when you open your mouth something quite different comes out, your man gives you a blank look, you try to put your thoughts into other words, but your emotions turn out to be mercurial, difficult to grasp. Here are articulations to help you pin them down in specific, clear language that shows your man you are trying to say something real and important to him after all, that what you've been struggling to share with him is not "secret women's stuff" that's beyond his ability—or that of *any* man—to comprehend.

Why am I the target if it's not me you're angry at?

You seem to be an angry sort of guy, but I'm attracted to your intensity, to your drive, to your yearning to be excellent. But you don't always know how to redirect your anger into constructive traits. Sometimes your anger becomes like a volcano about to erupt, and you end up blowing your top at me—even when it's not me you're angry at.

You file away little things I do that annoy you, and then when you have a fight with someone at work, or when something else that has nothing to do with me starts your clock ticking, you pack it up, bring it home, and take it out on me.

I may say, "Hi, honey," or something just as innocent, and the next thing I know you're jumping down my throat, attacking me for everything you can remember, and I feel like I'm living at the foot of Mount Vesuvius.

When you explode like that, maybe you just feel like kicking the dog, but I'm not the dog. If I do something that makes you angry, bring it up at the appropriate time—when I do it—not at some later date when the real cause of your current anger has nothing to do with me. I don't want to be your punching bag just because I happen to be convenient.

The next time something starts eating at you, instead of letting it build up inside you like a bomb, try talking it out with me. Who knows? Maybe you just need someone to listen to you. Maybe you'll find that the benefit of talking to me is not to hear me say a thing, but just to be able to listen to yourself and have a chance to blow off some steam.

It's time to get serious about taking me seriously.

I don't know if it's something about me personally or it's the fact that I'm a woman, or both—or what. But when I tell you things I strongly believe are important, you ignore me. And, not surprisingly, it bothers me!

It makes me angry when you trivialize what I have to say. By doing that, you put it—and *me*—down.

Can you understand how this could make me angry? Put yourself in my shoes. Imagine that you're telling me something important, and I sigh wearily—as if I'm bored—and turn my back on you. Or, the moment you've finished talking, instead of responding to what you've said, I completely change the subject to something that matters to *me*, as if what you just said isn't even worth a token response.

You wouldn't like that one bit, would you? Well, that's how you respond to me. So now I feel forced to make a formal request: *Start taking what I say seriously!* I don't want you to act for one minute more as if I'm incapable of a meaningful thought!

I don't think you really believe that, or you wouldn't have fallen in love with me. It's time to start acting like you know the truth.

I can't always swallow my anger to suit you—or even me.

Now and then angry emotions boil inside me. At times I can keep them on "simmer." But at other times I lose control. Yet the more I try to keep a lid on my feelings, the angrier I usually become. The anger turns to hostility, the hostility becomes hatred, and things start to get out of hand.

You don't like me to have fits of anger, I know. And maybe, at least part of the time, it *is* an over-reaction to some situation or comment you make.

But I'm not perfect. I never pretended I was. Right or wrong, I'm going to have occasional outbursts of anger. They're not something I can always control. Will you please expect it? Anticipate it? Factor it in? Understand? I realize it's an unpleasant experience for you. It's no picnic for me, either. I'll try not to make it a regular habit.

On the other hand, feeling free to explode on occasion has a constructive purpose. If I just keep my anger caged and seething inside me, I'd probably become sarcastic, cynical, and resentful, which of course neither of us wants.

So the next time I get angry at you—and sooner or later there will be a next time—will you remember we had this discussion and try to keep things in perspective? If you let me know it's okay to vent my feelings—even the angry ones—the sooner I can let go of them so that we can get on with our lives.

Everyone is entitled to be in a bad mood.

When I'm feeling down in the dumps, I appreciate your urge to do something concrete to make me feel better. The first thing to recognize is that it will pass. Eventually. It always does.

Meanwhile, though, the best thing you can do for me is not try to do too much.

I may just need to pour my heart out to you and feel free to burst into tears without you getting upset, even though I know you hate to see me cry. But it's just part of the process of working out my depression.

But sometimes what I need from you is just a simple hug. I may just feel alone and insecure. The touch of your arms, the feel of your warmth, just knowing you're physically and emotionally *there* for me, often helps me get grounded again.

However, there are also occasions when I feel sad, dejected, aimless, and inactive when you can't do *anything* for me. I have to help myself, and if that's the case, you need to recognize it, accept it, and give me space to bring myself back to normal. I may just lock myself in the bedroom and read for a while, or stare at the TV, or stare at the floor.

I realize that having me be blue is bad news, but the blues go as they come: unpredictably. When they hit, the most we both can do is try to see what's going on based on previous patterns and let me ride them out in whatever way feels most right at the time.

I wish I could always explain why I feel anxious.

I can't always put a label on the reasons for my anxiety. I wish I could. While no type of anxiety is pleasant, at least when the cause is apparent, the mixture of terror and despair seems easier to bear.

But sometimes I feel anxious for no reason that I can identify. That's the worst. Because if I don't know why I'm anxious, how can I predict when it will end? I feel like it'll never end. But when I try to explain *how* I feel to you, because I can't explain *why*—I have no examples; that's the point!—you don't take me seriously. That hurts.

When you treat this deeper, scarier, more profound form of anxiety like it doesn't exist because I can't tell you where it comes from, as if it were a city on a map, it only makes things worse. Do you think I *like* feeling a fear I can't even identify? It drives me crazy! Just being able to pinpoint its source would reduce the sense of threat that I feel hissing and crackling inside me like live wires.

When you don't acknowledge the genuineness of what I experience just because I can't articulate what it is, you only feed my sense of anxiety because I don't feel I can depend on you. Is it always important to *understand* why I feel anxious? Can't you just take my word that it's real and do your best to comfort me?

When I have a panic attack I really need your help.

There are times when I suddenly feel like I'm standing at the edge of a bottomless pit about to fall in. That's not ordinary anxiety. It's like looking Death in the face. Pow: everything stops. My head throbs. My heart pounds. My stomach knots. Every muscle in my body seems to tense up at once. My mind starts swirling with a blur of images that scares the hell out of me and I can't make it stop.

When I feel like that, I need you to be there for me more than at any other time. My world is collapsing like a house of cards. I'm dying inside. What I don't need and really can't handle at times like those is having you ignore me or just go off somewhere to leave me alone.

When I tell you I'm in a state of panic, will you recognize that inside me, earthquakes are sending shock waves through me and there's no more urgent time that I need your support? If you really love me, that's when I need you to show it. Do you love me *that* much?

Do you know what my biggest fear is? Uncertainty.

I wish I knew what my future will be. I have no idea what I'm going to do with the rest of my life, where I'm heading, if any of the dreams I cherished as a child are ever going to come true.

I feel like I'm floundering. I feel directionless. I don't feel like I have a clear purpose in life. Everything just seems so iffy, so up in the air.

But still, with you at my side, I might be able to start accepting that the worst that could possibly happen isn't so bad, and that I can take control of my life. You may not be able to help me completely conquer my fear of the unknown, but you can help me feel a lot less scared just by letting me know that you're behind me, giving me emotional support, loving me no matter what.

Will you do that? Will you let me know from time to time? Even if it's just a word of confidence, even if you just give me a hug when you sense my worry, I could take heart from that and it would make me feel more secure.

I just looked in the mirror and you know what I saw? You dumping me.

I'm getting older. My bustline is starting to drop. My hips are starting to spread. My hair is getting grayer strand by strand. Little wrinkles are forming at the corners of my eyes like bird tracks on a sandy beach. And it frightens and upsets me.

I need to hear you say that you still find me attractive—if you do. I need to hear the sincerity in your voice. I don't like growing older any more than you do, but I think it might be easier for a man. A man's looks don't seem to change quite so radically overnight. And who's kidding whom? No matter what I, or anybody else, may say in a more confident moment, looks are important to most of us most of the time. Especially to a woman.

I'm feeling very vulnerable right now, so would you talk to me from your heart and tell me what I mean to you? I think I'd feel better knowing that beauty is in the eye of the beholder and that in your eyes I'm still as pretty as the girl you first met.

Just because some guy touches my arm, it doesn't mean we're sleeping together—or want to.

I don't want to fight about this subject anymore, okay?

Is it *you* who's fooling around? Is that it? Are you thinking about it? Are you taking *your* guilt and attributing it to me?

I don't know if it's true—I certainly hope not—but I can't help but give it serious thought because of the irrational ways you act. Your insecurity about my "unfaithfulness" has no basis in fact.

Yes, I find some guys attractive, and they feel the same. *You* were one of them, remember? Do you think you're the only man on earth who thinks I'm attractive and personable? You're not. But you are the *only* man for me. I refuse to lock myself up in the house because you can't accept that. It's the truth.

Sure, I may flirt a little at parties. Don't you? Doesn't everyone, just a little? It's normal. It doesn't mean anything. This isn't *Dallas* or *Dynasty*. This isn't a soap opera. It's real life. Flirting is fun. It's harmless. It's just one way people relate when they're together and feeling comfortable and relaxed.

But that's *all* it is. There's no foundation for conjuring up visions of secret trysts. You're making much ado about nothing. Unless, that is, the fuss really has to do with you. Does it? Be honest. I'm telling you now for the last time it doesn't have to do with me.

In any event, it might be a good idea if you and I talked. Because your jealousy is getting out of control. It makes people uncomfortable. It makes me edgy, too. What's *really* behind it?

Hey, tough guy, don't say, "Don't worry about me."

I'm the one who loves you. I'm *supposed* to worry about you. Isn't that what people who love each other do? You bet it is! I want you to worry about me, too.

Furthermore, I *want* you to know that I'm concerned about you. I'm not saying that when you're not around I think about you every second, but when you don't show up at a time when I expect you, I start to imagine all sorts of dire things. Would you please be more thoughtful and call me so I won't expect the worst? I can't help it. That's how my mind works. And it's not because I'm neurotic, either, or some scaredy-cat—you know better.

It's because I care about you very much, even though I know you can take care of yourself.

When I share my concerns about you with you, and you casually dismiss them, you may think you're telling me not to worry. But the real message you're giving is "Stop caring about me." I don't think you realize that.

You do want me to care about you, don't you? I certainly want you to care about me.

Women aren't the only ones who are moody.

You think women are unstable, flighty, mercurial, whimsical, contradictory, crazy, weird, and a lot of other unserious stuff, just because women show their moods.

But men are moody, too. Even you. You may not verbalize your moods as much as I do, but you show them in other ways.

By being silent when something is clearly eating at you.

By getting furious over some little thing.

By making demands. My dictator, with our house like your country. Me—a population of one. And you—why, at times I think I should sew gold-braided epaulets on your bathrobe.

If you think about it, you'll see that you're just as emotional as I am, even though I may show my emotions differently, the way women are brought up to do. The difference is that I externalize more what's going on inside me. You keep your feelings under lock and key.

But that doesn't mean you don't have feelings. You do. They're there. If you want to go on pretending they don't exist—well, that's up to you. But I know you better than that. And you know better, too.

Would you please not interrupt me when I'm talking?

I wish we could tape-record what happens when I try to say something to you. You step on my words. You cut me off in mid-sentence. You act as if you can't wait for me to be quiet so you can say something that *really* matters.

Hey, my existence counts, too. What I say *matters*. It matters to my colleagues at work. It matters to my friends. It matters to my family. It's mattered to the men in my life before you. I expect it to matter to you.

When you talk, I listen. I don't interrupt. Sometimes you say things that I disagree with, or things I don't really think even *you* believe, but still I hear you out with at least a modicum of civility, consideration, and common politeness.

All I'm asking is that you treat me with equal respect.

V

GROWTH

How do you talk to a man about issues that neither of you may ever have broached before, not because you wouldn't like to, but because it never was obvious to you that they could *be* suitable subjects for discussion? Like a need you may feel for self-improvement. Or a feeling of stagnation, if your relationship has stopped evolving. Or a feeling of concern that you and your man are drifting apart. Here is a set of easy ways to raise such major themes that wend their way through your relationship not just now but always. Use these articulations to keep your man in touch with you—and vice versa—as you grow together into your future.

I want you to nurture me the way only a man can.

There seems to be a widespread perception that nurturing is reserved for women. Men get it, women give it, and women don't need nurturing in return.

That just ain't so.

I need you to tell me—sincerely—that I'm good at my job when I feel like a failure.

I need you to encourage me to talk—by listening—even if you can't understand half the things I say. If you care enough to keep listening, eventually you'll understand.

I need you to put your arms around me when I feel scared, and remind me that the two of us together can lick anything.

I need you to appreciate that your role in this relationship is not just to handle the major crises. It's also to care about little things because I care about them and you care about me.

And even if I do something terrific, I still need you to tell me, "I'm proud of you." Because your opinion means that much to me.

I want us to have something to show for our relationship.

Together we've grown a good deal. We've loved, we've fought, we've made up, we've struggled to understand each other, we've worked together side by side, we've experienced joys as a couple, and we've had our share of sorrows too.

And yet, for all the emotional energy we've put into it, our relationship is still invisible. We take each day as it comes, and that's fine, but I wish we had a plan for the future as well, something hard and solid and three-dimensional that we, and everybody else, can see. Something that we can take special pride in because it's a tangible creation we made as a couple, something, in fact, that could symbolize our relationship.

Maybe it's starting to save for a house.

Maybe it's starting a business together.

Maybe it's starting a garden in the backyard.

Whatever it is, I need it to be something I can physically see, a goal we achieved together and enjoyed doing, that made sense to do. Something we can feel represents not just you or me but *us*.

Any suggestions?

You act like Cary Grant in public and Archie Bunker at home.

Isn't it time you stopped doing the little things you know annoy me (because I point them out to you)? If you did them in public, I would feel embarrassed, but at least your behavior would be consistent and I would have to say to myself, "Look, that's just the way he is."

But you don't leave the toilet seat up when you go to the john in someone else's home.

You don't belch out loud at the dinner table with other people around—even if those people are in our home as guests.

You don't lean over your food, wielding your knife and fork like weapons, wolfing down whatever's on your plate, as if someone were going to steal it from you.

In fact, sometimes you astonish me with how polite and elegantly mannered you *can* be.

You seem to have a double standard of behavior: a quite astonishing and civilized standard when you're in public, and something completely opposite when you're with me.

You say you're just feeling free to be comfortable and to be yourself when I'm around, that in public you feel you have to be "on." Okay, I can understand that. But when you do something like burp out loud during a meal, it isn't funny. It makes me lose my appetite. And especially after I've asked you not to do it, it makes me think that you're not really committed to us as a couple, because my feelings don't count for too much. And I don't think that's what you want.

Howdy, stranger.

Me and Ole Paint here been ridin' the range for a powerful long time without seein' hide nor hair of another human bein' and I gotta tell ya, partner, it's mighty lonely by yourself out there on the plain, with only prairie dogs and coyotes for company.

Ain't you and I supposed to be ridin' together on this cow-trail of life? Didn't we have that understanding between us? 'Cause the last time we sat down to slug some tequila or play a few hands of stud poker or ride on into town to kick up our heels feels like afore the Civil War.

What I'm a tryin' to say is, you're my guy and I'm your gal and we ain't actin' like it. We ain't doin' what nature intended. We hardly even spend any time with each other. I'm startin' to feel like we're on opposite sides of the Great Divide.

What say we climb down to the bottom and meet in the middle for a powwow about our relationship and how we can find some more time to spend being *in* it?

When I imagined finding someone and falling in love, this wasn't exactly what I had in mind.

It's funny, but I'd always pictured myself with a man quite different from you, an idealized fantasy of a man. He was six feet tall and built like an aerobics instructor. He looked like an actor but had the mind of a scientist.

And yet, my Mr. Perfect was not consumed by his work. He had plenty of spare time for other things. He might dabble in the stock market and make $10 million—just for the fun of it; he didn't care about the money. He might try sculpting as a hobby, and prestigious galleries would display his art. A novel he dashed off just to amuse himself would become a bestseller and then be made into a movie.

Of course he'd be the perfect lover and would know just the right thing to do for me in every situation before I knew myself.

In other words, he was about as real as Batman.

Even so, it's hard to let go of those childhood fantasies. It's tough to accept that perfect men don't exist, or perfect women— that it's just not in the nature of human beings to be without flaws.

And part of me knows that if my fantasy man magically materialized, I would hate it. He'd be perfect; I'd still be me.

You may not be my fantasy man, but I wouldn't trade you for him even if I could. Still, I've held onto that impossibly perfect vision for so many years that it's etched on my consciousness. It's probably going to take some time before it totally fades away.

I'm not asking you to do anything. This is just a little secret something about me that I wanted you to know because I love you, and I want to share as much about myself with you as I can.

Let's reach out and touch someone: each other.

Don't you feel like we're getting too complacent about our relationship? I do. I don't want us to stay together just because we've become a mutual habit that's simply easier to continue than quit. Shouldn't we have a reason to keep on being part of a couple? Shouldn't that reason be because it's something we both honestly, actively want?

I would like to feel that we're genuinely growing together as a result of being together, not merely treading water. I want us to find some new ways to learn how to enjoy each other more, rather than let the fresh, natural, spontaneous, and alive feelings we initially felt continue to fade due to neglect.

Maybe, just to get the ball rolling, we need a project, something we've never done before, something we can do together less for the thing itself than to rediscover the happiness or the contentment of feeling part of a team. A trip, for instance. Or some new experience. An adventure. Or some worthwhile project that we can get involved in as partners, working together toward a common goal, so that we can re-experience the fulfillment and reward of evolving together and reminding us of our love.

Because I *do* love you, and I think you still love me. But I wish we could start acting like it a little more, and there's no reason why we can't. We've just let ourselves get lazy, that's all. But I've looked at myself and thought, "Hey, I've got plenty of energy left for our relationship." Don't you? Come on, you know you do. Let's find our second wind.

Are we still a couple or two ships passing in the night?

Since I've been alone for a good part of my life, it's safe to say I know what that's like. I also remember quite clearly how and when we first met, and how fantastic it was to fall in love with you and become a couple.

But something's happening. Maybe it's happening slowly, but it's there, barely detectable at first but becoming more pronounced each day—at least for me. We're becoming more like roommates than lovers. We share the same living space, but otherwise our lives are becoming more and more filled with other people and other things to do so that there's less and less time for us. We've both been developing a case of preoccupation and I don't want it to become chronic. Even that possibility makes me think twice about our future. Do we really have one? The answer isn't as obvious now as I once thought.

I may not be alone—literally—the way I was before I met you, but I no longer feel quite like part of a couple these days, either. Little by little, we're allowing our relationship to erode. We're letting ourselves drift further and further apart.

Do you know what I think the loneliest feeling is? It's not being physically alone. It's *feeling* alone in a crowded room, or even a room where there's just one other person—especially if that person is the man you're supposed to love and care about, and who's supposed to feel the same about you.

I feel that kind of loneliness creeping over me. I don't like it. I want to do something about it. I need your help.

I always thought our love would grow. It seems to me that we've been stuck in the same place for a long time.

Our relationship is stagnating. We always seem to be busy with something or someone other than each other. And for the few moments we *are* together at home, we're too exhausted to really relate.

This can't go on—at least not for me. We need to recommit ourselves to each other if our relationship is going to survive. We need to reaffirm by actions and by words that we truly do care about each other, because love doesn't stand still. It grows or it fades. And our love needs to start growing—now—or it will surely disappear.

What we have at the moment is a kind of holding action. Is it fulfilling to you? I doubt it. It sure isn't meeting my needs. Personally, I'd like to get off my butt and start doing something about it, but I can't revitalize us without you, and I realize now that it's not going to happen by an act of God. We're going to have to make it happen—together.

I'm ready to try. I'm prepared to work real hard to make our relationship work. Consider this an invitation to join me. It's a formal invitation—with an R.S.V.P.

I need you to accept—and appreciate—that I'm not the same woman you first met.

I've been acting differently lately and it has upset and confused you. Let me try to explain what's going on.

We met. We fell in love. Time passed. You changed. I changed, too. Some of my changes were obvious, but you know, most of the obvious changes were really little things. But other things—big things—were changing inside me, slowly, invisibly, and it wasn't always clear to *me* what was going on. I just knew it was something, and I waited for whatever it was to sort itself out and become clear so that I could say to myself, "Okay, this is what seems to be happening. Here's what I should do next."

I'm *growing*. And whether it feels good to you or not, whether it makes you feel uncertain or not, whether you want it to happen or not, it's going to happen anyway. It's a natural process of life.

Frankly, I don't want to change it, but even if I did, I couldn't. It would be like trying to suffocate myself. This is how I am *now*. I feel like a new flower just starting to unfold. I don't know who I'm becoming, but it feels right to me. And I think, I hope—no, I actually am *confident*—that it will be a good thing for both of us. In the long run.

So, please, don't fight it. Change is good. Accept it. Appreciate it. Let it happen.

δδ

___

I've decided to make an investment in myself.

I have a powerful need to learn something new. I feel like my mind has begun to atrophy, and that it's capable of handling a lot more—understanding a lot more—but that I've allowed it to grow weak and flabby with disuse, or not enough mentally taxing use.

So I'm going to go back to school, or maybe start by taking an adult education course, or join a club, or begin a hobby: something for me and me alone, something to improve myself and make me feel better about myself.

You may think I'm fine the way I am, and I appreciate that. You may not want to risk having me change, and I can understand that. But I'd like you to look beyond those feelings and support me in this learning experience I need to go through.

I'll need your support. It will cost money—not a lot, but some. It will take time—and I don't know how much. Yet. Maybe a lot. But I'll try to keep it economical. I'll do my very best to make sure you don't feel like you're suddenly taking a back seat to something else in my life, because I wouldn't want that. But it's likely that the time we'll be spending together at least for a while will be more quality time and less quantity time. That may take some adjusting to. But if you meet me halfway, I'm sure we can work it out.

If I had my wish, I'd hope you'd think of my new direction like this: that I'm taking your most important asset and increasing its value. How about that?

When I see other couples split up, it scares me.

It reminds me that it could happen to us. I want to prevent that. I know there are no guarantees in this life. But I also get the feeling that you haven't quite committed yourself body and soul to our relationship, that a part of you is being held in reserve, a part that says, "Well, she may be okay for now, until someone really right for me comes along."

That shred of doubt I sense in you frightens me. One minute I think we're building something solid and secure together. The next, it seems like I'm living in a house of cards.

Do you have doubts? Because if you don't, I want to know that when you dream about the future, that dream includes me.

Why can't you just accept me for who I am?

It's taken me a long time to learn how to like myself and I don't appreciate the ways you try to make me different, presumably better, as if I weren't good enough the way I am.

When you ask me to have my hair done a certain way or to wear certain kinds of clothes because it will make me look more feminine, that really hurts.

When you want to know why I'm not more like so-and-so's girlfriend, I think, "He's comparing me to her and he thinks I don't measure up."

Is that what you think? Because I'm the same woman you fell in love with. Yes, I've changed a little over time but I'm substantially the same, I think. *You're* the one who's changing—in your attitudes toward me.

If I'm not good enough for you, just tell me. Sure it would hurt but no more than this. At least then I'd know exactly why you were chipping away at me.

Otherwise, I want you to start loving me for who I am, not who you wish I could be.

I'm afraid if I do what I really want to do it will push us apart.

I've invested my whole self in this relationship. I've put my other needs for self-definition and self-worth on a back burner, and as a result, I've become less forthright in telling you what's really on my mind—more one-dimensional, and less interesting in general. I want to change, but I have a feeling you won't like it and that it might signal the end of the relationship.

Don't you find me boring? I know I find myself bored. All my free thoughts, all my free time have been poured into *us*, into pleasing you. Now I see there's not very much of *me* left anymore. There's only *us*.

I'm not sorry for all the energy I put into being a couple, but now I realize it's time for me to concentrate on *me*. To do something I want to do for a change, not for us, not for you, but to make my life more interesting for me.

But I'm wary. I'm sure you've forgotten what I was like as an individual. It seems like we've always been a couple. And as intent as I am on recovering the *me* in *us*, I'm afraid it will cause friction around here.

I need to hear you tell me that *I'm* as important as *we* are. Can you let me know you'll understand and that although we'll be together in a new way, with a new me, we'll still be together?

I'm not a girl just like the girl who married dear old Dad.

It's said that we become our parents. In some ways I suppose that's true. As we get older, we start to pick up our parents' way of doing things more and more.

I notice you becoming increasingly like your father. And the more you start to resemble your dad, the more you start to pressure me—in little ways—to act like your mom.

I'm asking you to stop it, please. Now.

I'm sure your mother was a wonderful woman when you were growing up. But I'm not her. I'll never be her. I don't want to be her. And I don't want you to want me to be her.

I want you to want me to be me. You're supposed to love me for who *I* am, not for the things I may do—or that you may want me to do—that remind you of your mom.

Would you let me be me and not try to turn me into someone else?

I want to take more chances but I need you to stand by me.

Now that the excitement of discovery that's part of infatuation is behind us, do you know what the most important benefit of being with you in a relationship is for me? It's your strength. It's the potential for me to be able to take chances with my life, knowing that I've got a person, a man, a strong individual—you—to support me emotionally. It minimizes my fear of failing, and that, I think, is the deepest, most terrible fear of all: failing and being disdained and rejected and rebuked because I wasn't better, because I didn't succeed, because I wasn't perfect.

There. I've said it. I'm terrified of taking risks. Oh, I'll take them all right. But I always feel torn. I want a better job. I'll fight like a tiger to get a promotion, but then if I actually get it, I think, "Oh my God, what have I done? I can't handle this! I'll drop the ball, fall on my face, and a bolt of lightning will shoot out of the sky and strike me dead!"

Don't smile! I actually think stuff like this!

You, I might add, are no help. And you could be. I need you to be. Even though I put on a brave front, now that you know what's behind my attempt to look like Mother Courage, would you recognize that I'm scared? Take the initiative and say to me: "Darling, I want you to succeed, but even if you're an abject failure, even if you feel like a complete fool, even if you want to die of embarrassment, I'll still love you. I'm behind you all the way. I'll help you pick yourself up off the ground. Whatever else you decide to do, you can count on me."

VI

LIFE

Many people don't make anything of their lives together. They allow themselves to live with each other with no real sense of direction, of shared purpose. No wonder there are so many divorces. No wonder so many people are unable to commit to a long-term relationship. They never quite get around to talking about what their goals are. Or how their values are changing. Or even whether they're still happy with each other. These articulations will help you start discussions about some of the most important issues in your life—because they are *about* life—your life, your man's life, what each of you wants out of life as individuals and as a couple. These are issues that too many people take for granted. While no one solution is right for everyone, the answers begin with regular conversations about life, conversations that this chapter will help you have again and again

Once I'd have killed to be rich. Now I'd only maim.

For a good part of my life I thought—not always consciously—"You are what you own." And other people owned what I wanted. I coveted things out of my reach. An elegant home. A Mercedes. Diamonds. Furs. Designer clothes. Extended vacations in exotic places. Even people, if they were glamorous, I saw as a reflection of me; I wanted to be in the "right" crowd. All these status symbols were important to the person I was going to become.

Well, I'm still evolving, of course, but I already *have* become someone. She isn't the person I imagined, but she's still pretty nice, I think. I really like myself. Now, I don't need a penthouse or jewels or sables to bolster my sense of self-esteem and to know that I'm worthwhile.

I've learned values. I've got ethics. There are lines I'd no longer cross just to get ahead.

But if you insist on buying me a diamond-encrusted Piaget watch—by all means, don't let me stop you.

Why are we still keeping up with the Joneses?

I'm getting sick of expressing who I am through material objects. And why does it usually have to be something somebody else has?

Aren't you getting a little fed up with going through life as if you were playing Monopoly for real?

Gotta get Park Place and Boardwalk.

Gotta get enough money to build houses.

Gotta hope somebody has a bad toss of dice so that he lands on one of them so you can build more houses, and then hotels.

Gotta hope he has another bad throw before we land on his properties with hotels.

Gotta bankrupt him before he bankrupts us.

Gotta kill or be killed. Victory at any price. Prove we're good-better-best.

Gotta-gotta-gotta.

You know what the problem with the rat race is? Even if you win it you're still a rat.

Can't we stop competing with our friends, the people at your office, the people where I work, the neighbors, our relatives, and the characters on TV in L.A. *Law*? When someone asks me my name, I'm starting to feel like I should say Bloomingdale's or American Express, take your pick.

Is there a real point to all this? Or is it just our way of telling the world that we're insecure?

It's true: What you look like, you are.

You know, you really are cheap. Instead of springing for a few extra bucks to get the best, you're always buying second-rate stuff. Stuff that doesn't last, that has no enduring quality, that might as well carry a price tag that says, "This is inferior, cheap, and low-class."

Like it or not, people judge you by what you have, what you wear, how you look: every little detail about your life that becomes part of your image. You say you don't care what people think. Well, I do, and I suspect that you do, too.

For a guy who's accomplished as much as you have, when you walk around in those moth-eaten clothes—the first real "business" suit you ever got or that coat that looks like it came out of your grandfather's closet—nobody would believe it.

Maybe you think it's okay to look like you aren't successful, but I don't like it and it makes our friends uncomfortable, because they're successful and they assumed you were, too—until they got a gander at all this cheap junk.

Let's start looking, acting, and living like we can really afford. I've got nothing against saving money for a rainy day, but you act like you're building an ark. Come on. Open a coffer. Spend a few shillings, shekels, or yen. Who knows? You may actually enjoy it. Most people do.

Diamonds are still a girl's best friend.

My grandmother always said, about jewelry, "Don't wear anything unless it's real." A fourteen-carat gold bracelet rather than a gold-colored or gold-plated one.

Well, instead of having a boxful of costume jewelry, I'd like to have one genuine thing.

A diamond. A ring.

Or two things. Diamond earrings.

Or three things or more. A bracelet, a necklace. Be imaginative!

Show me you love me. Buy me a diamond. A real one. One that I can scratch glass with.

A diamond is enduring. So am I. But can you endure me on your case all the time?

Be nice. Shut me up. Buy me a piece of the rock.

Say, are we perfect yet?

How would you rate us as a couple? Would you give us four stars? Do you think we're better off than our friends?

I've been thinking about that lately—not just things we own but also the quality of our life together. And our careers. And what we bring to our togetherness as people.

So, I put it to you. Are we proud of ourselves? Are we pleased with our accomplishments? Should we be? Questions like these have been nagging at me. I'm not sure what the answers are. Are you? Could you run down this list with me to see if we can figure out where we're at?

- Can you think of three words to describe us?
- Did we meet any of our goals? Did we *have* any goals? Is it too late to set some?
- What else do we want from our life together?
- What are we working toward?
- Are we happy?

I think we've done pretty well, myself. And I think we should give ourselves a pat on the back. But I also think we should keep these questions in mind and bring them up every now and then. What do you think?

I don't have half the things I always wanted, but I just realized that I don't feel deprived.

Hey, you know, it's the strangest thing. I feel like I just woke up after having the longest dream. All my life I wanted and wanted and wanted things. And I had to work and work and work to get them. Because that's what I always thought life was about, wanting and wanting, and working and working, and then wanting more; an endless cycle.

Now, suddenly, the list of "gotta-haves" in my mind has diminished, and I'm noticing it for the first time. There isn't anything I need that I don't have, and there isn't anything I want that I need. I don't know exactly how it happened, but I'm happy. I don't mean I'm deliriously, ecstatically happy, but I'm content. I feel fulfilled. And I feel kind of lucky.

I may not have half the things I always wanted, but I've got you.

You're not the only one who's made sacrifices to get us where we are today.

Thank you, my Aztec slave.

Thank you, my builder of pyramids, my bringer of fire, my road warrior, my Joan of Arc, my Socrates, my Robert E. Lee, my Ollie North, my Tammy Bakker, my Rin Tin Tin, my Benji.

Thank you, oh thank you, again and again, for everything I owe you: my looks, my health, all my worldly goods, the thrill of shopping for food for you, the ecstasy of picking up the clothes you leave strewn on the floor, the bliss of being by your side when you come home from work after a bad day and take it out on me.

Ah, living with you is pure heaven. So thanks, merci, gracias, and xie xie (which is Chinese: We aim to please). I'm so grateful and thankful to you for all the sacrifices you've made and continue to make for me every single waking hour of your miserable wretched life that to hear you complain about *you*, what *you've* done, and what *you've* given up for the sake of us nearly makes me forget that I've made just as many sacrifices as you—if not more!

I could give you a litany of all the things I've left behind, given up, done without, put out of my mind, lived with, endured, suffered, prevailed over, scaled, assaulted, warded off, and hexed to make this relationship work.

I will, if you insist. It wouldn't be any *less* boring than your litany, at least I can guarantee that. But I shouldn't have to recount my sacrifices to prove my list is as long as yours and that each item on it carries equal weight. Wake up. Look around you. I'm not saying you haven't paid dues, but we're both lifetime members of the same club.

We talk about kids today not having any values, but sometimes I wonder about us.

What are our ethics?

What do we consider right and wrong?

Do we as a couple have a social conscience?

These are weird times. Where do we stand on the issues. What *are* the issues? There seems to be so many. Do we have to take a stand on *all* of them? And if we don't, how do we decide which ones to adopt as our causes and which to drop because we just don't have the time?

I worry that we may be selfish. What about the homeless people we see every day in the street? What about AIDS victims? What about the elderly? The poor? The physically handicapped? The mentally handicapped?

Where is our contribution to making this a better world? Maybe we ought to give some serious thought to doing volunteer work. I'm not saying that we alone can cure the world of its ills, but let's not get so overwhelmed that we just shut out what's there in front of our eyes. Let's pick one thing, one decent worthwhile cause and get involved in making a difference—to others and to ourselves.

Is your God better than mine?

We've been through all this before. The answer then was no. It's still no.

Worshipping God (or not) is a very personal thing. You do it your way. I'll do it mine.

Let's get religion.

There's something missing in our lives. We're so focussed on relating to each other that we've overlooked an important aspect of relating to our world. I'm talking about religion. Spirituality. God.

A belief in God, and a spiritual life, can add a wider perspective and a feeling of belonging to what we already have.

I want us to remember that there is an ancient but active pattern of ritual that has long preceded us and that will continue long after we are gone. You and I can become part of an enormous family, celebrating, observing, and growing through our faith.

I want to learn to understand myself better. I want you to learn to understand yourself and how we both fit into this order, this world.

I think worship can help us do that. Will you worship with me for my sake, if not for yours?

I've thought about leaving you.

I've packed my bags a hundred times in my mind. I've realized that running away won't solve our problems. But I still think about it, and I'm thinking about it now.

I'm not trying to threaten you, but when I try to talk to you about ways in which we might change our relationship for the better, you say something like, "Don't worry. Things'll work out." And then we go on as before, things don't work out, and again, mentally, I start packing my bags.

What I'm saying to you now is that you should worry. It isn't written in the stars that I'll stay with you forever if our problems don't improve. I realize that our difficulties—not the least of which is lack of communication—don't just have to do with you. I've played a part as well. There are things I've wanted to share with you and haven't because I just felt I never could, and so I never tried. Things like that are my fault, not yours.

Rather than replay this fantasy I have of leaving you yet again, can we please sit down and have a heart-to-heart talk about commitment in a relationship and what it means to each of us? I think a talk like that is long past due.

I'm disappointed.

Disappointment has been building up in me about us for a long time. Our life together is not turning out the way I had planned.

Maybe I had unrealistic expectations. Maybe I thought that you were the knight in shining armor who would change my life so completely that the rest of our life together would be like a fairy tale. Maybe it's the promises you made and didn't keep, or the things we said we'd do and never did, or the places we'd planned to go and never went, things we said we'd buy and never quite saved up enough to get.

Or maybe I'm just getting older, becoming more pragmatic, maturing, and seeing life for what it is in reality. But I have this overwhelming sense of despair. I feel like I let myself down. I feel like I let you down. I feel like you let me down. Life itself feels like one big letdown.

But is that it? Are we beyond hope? Can't we do something to shake this pessimistic attitude? I don't want us to break up—at least I don't think I do.

I'd like to take a stab at carving a new life for ourselves, of hoisting ourselves out of this rut of unfulfilled desires. But I can't do it alone. Will you join me in trying to rise above the disappointments and into a more positive, optimistic, and rewarding relationship for us both?

Say, how about a hand? And I don't mean applause!

How come I end up doing most of the chores around here? I put in a full day on the job just like you. And yet I end up shopping for groceries, cooking dinner, doing the dishes afterward, vacuuming the living room, dusting, scouring the bathroom—I'm starting to feel like Cinderella before she met the prince.

You're supposed to be my prince. But I feel like your serf. Come on. Start pitching in. Make dinner once in a while. I know you don't like it. Nobody likes it. But if you don't want to go hungry, somebody's got to do it. You should feel just a little embarrassed and ashamed that you don't lift a finger to help out around the house. It's not my job just because I'm a woman. I get dressed up each morning and go to work. That's my job. This is drudgery, and I wouldn't mind doing it half as much if I had a guy who cared enough to lend a hand.

So, starting tomorrow, consider yourself drafted.

VII

HEALTH

Nobody really believes "If you have your health you have everything"—until it's lost. Suddenly everything else in life comes to a screeching halt. On the other hand, we're much more conscious of the need to safeguard our health now than we ever were in times past—and we're more knowledgeable about how to do that—so it's become more acceptable, even more fashionable, for a couple to discuss health just as naturally as they discuss any other important concern. That's what these articulations provide: an easy entry into some of the most important health issues you and your man may need to talk out. Do you want to lose weight? Does he drink too much? Could you both use a vacation to renew yourselves? What you won't find in here is answers. What you will find are the beginnings of conversations it might do you good to have.

Smoking isn't cool anymore.

Isn't that why you first lit up in junior high? Because you wanted to look tough? Because you wanted to look cool? Because it felt sexy? Because you wanted to fit in?

Well, maybe as a kid you felt like you were going to live forever or didn't even know that smoking could kill you, but now you know.

I'm asking you to stop smoking because it can give you cancer, heart disease, emphysema, and a lot of other scary stuff.

I'm asking you to stop smoking because just being around you when you smoke makes me a passive smoker, and even though I know you don't mean it, you may be hurting me.

I'm asking you to stop smoking because it gives you bad breath, and it makes your teeth yellow and unattractive, and it leaves ugly nicotine stains on your fingers.

I'm asking you to quit because other people don't like it. In restaurants, they give us cold stares, or whisper among themselves, or complain to the maître d'.

If you can't—or won't—commit yourself to kicking the habit for the sake of living longer, kick it because you're a nice guy who likes people, and *they* can't stand it when you smoke.

Think back to that very first cigarette, the circumstances, *why* you lit up. Remember the *real* reason. Doesn't it seem ridiculous now? You know the answer.

Quit. Now. Before you make yourself sick. That definitely isn't cool.

It's time to admit you don't have a "drinking problem." You're an alcoholic.

We've had this discussion before. Countless times. That's not what this is about. This is a Western Union telegram from me to you. It says:

Urgent!
AA HAS BEEN CONTACTED ON YOUR BEHALF.
THEY'RE WAITING FOR YOU TO CALL. NOW.

Yes, I made that phone call and spoke to AA. They want to speak with you. But you have to make the first move. They want to help. Call them back. Either do what they say or I'm out of here. I love you but I've had it. I can't take any more.

Do you want to be a drunk and be alone, or do you want me around to help you kick this thing—this disease? If you want my help, fine. Take it. I'm the one who requested this phone call. I expect you to pick up the receiver and start talking this thing out.

I don't want a guy who can't have a good time unless he's high.

When you get high, even though you're sitting next to me, you're not with me. You're lost in your own little world and I feel left out.

But what really bothers me is when we make love, because even though I know you enjoy the heightened sensory feeling of being stoned when you have sex, I don't feel you're having sex with me: the separate, distinct, unique human being you're supposed to love. You could be with *any* woman. Precisely because your senses get abnormally magnified and your mind is flashing a whole thought-stream of images, you aren't able to focus on any one thing. Including me.

When we're together, especially when we're together in bed, I want you to really be *there* with me, not just in body but also in mind. That's what having a relationship is about.

Right now it seems to me that the only relationship you're having is with the drug of your choice. Dump the dope. Be with me instead. You can't do both.

I'm going into "weight training" and I need a good coach.

It's time for us both to admit that I could lose a few pounds. Each time I look in the mirror, each time I see fattening food, it's the first thing that flashes across my mind: I need to get on a diet—a simple, no-nonsense, non-fad, medically approved plan for eating and living—fewer calories, the right foods, some sort of regular exercise. And commit to it. Not for a month. Not for six months. Not for a year. *For life.*

There, I've said the awful truth: If you want real results, dieting isn't temporary. That's just torture. A real diet does not promise instant, dramatic change. A real diet is like getting married. It's something you promise to love, honor, and obey until death do us part. It's for keeps.

But now that you see how my mind is made up, I'll need your support. Determined as I am to diet, I know full well how tough it is to truly change, especially when it's something as fundamental as the way I eat every single day. If I know me, I'll go through a period when I'll think about fattening food every waking moment without letting myself indulge.

Agony!

But this is a life decision I've made. And because I have to do it for real, I need your cooperation. When you see me glance at the fridge in a moment of weakness, clear your throat. When you see that food-crazed look on my face, rustle the newspaper. Do some little thing to *remind* me. And don't sabotage my efforts by tempting me with foods you know I love and must avoid.

Will you give me a hand? Will you keep me true to myself? Will you be my coach and conscience? When I'm slimmer, we'll both get off on how good I look. I know you won't love me more or less because of what I weigh, but I'll feel better about me and so will you.

It upsets me that you don't care enough about yourself to eat right.

Once, it seemed you could eat anything. Nobody worried about gaining weight or otherwise endangering their health. That didn't mean we were safe. It meant we were blissfully ignorant. We didn't really know that careless eating could shorten your life—in fact, *cut* it short.

Now we know.

I want us to start eating right. We'll do it together: you and I. I won't try to tell you that good, *healthful* food is as tasty as some of our favorite treats, but we can make good food taste good enough so you feel like you're eating *real* food.

But the point is *living longer.*

When you think about that and how you can do that by changing the way you eat, and then *do* it, you'll feel better about yourself. Each time you sit down to eat, part of you will feel good that you care about who you are.

Don't you want that? I want that. I want to have you around for a long time.

Exercise! Or you'll break both our hearts!

Take exercise seriously because living is a serious business. I've heard you use every excuse. No time. You don't want to spend the money. It makes your muscles sore. And on and on.

No more excuses, okay?

You owe it to us to get your act together exercise-wise. And stick to a regular fitness program. Whether it's swimming, cycling, jogging, a martial art, or some combination of things is academic. *Do something!*

Take a walk! What could be easier? Go out for a half-hour and stride through the neighborhood. Today people walk as a serious thing. You could get some walking shoes and a spiffy outfit. Walkers even have their own magazines.

You've got plenty of choices. Pick something.

I don't want you hurting your health, especially your heart. And since regular exercise burns off stress as well as calories, you'll leave the tensions of work where they belong—at the job—and not bring them home to me.

Not only that, but once your body gets adjusted, which may only take a week or two, exercise gives you plenty of pep and vigor. It makes you feel good. It makes you feel more alive. It'll put you in a better mood. That'll put *me* in a better mood.

So do us both a favor.

Shake it!

Why won't you get a checkup?

You don't have to be sick to see a doctor these days. You only have to see a doctor one lousy time a year and you make a big deal out of it. You say you feel fine. *Fine!* That's when you're supposed to get a medical checkup, to make sure you *stay* in good health.

Or is it something else? Are you afraid you'll hear something you don't want to hear? That doesn't make sense. Since when do you take an ostrich-with-its-head-in-the-sand attitude toward life? Show a little courage. If you feel fine, you probably are fine. Won't it feel better just to know for sure?

And don't complain about the money it costs. Splurge! If you have to spend money on something, what better thing to invest in than preventive medicine. This is your life we're talking about! What's that worth? I say everything—at the very least the fifty or a hundred dollars a doctor will charge to check you out.

Cars need a tune-up every fifty thousand miles and people need a checkup once a year. Don't be stubborn. Don't you owe it to yourself to treat yourself as well as you treat a machine? Pick up the phone. Make an appointment. Do it now.

Doctors are busy these days because everybody's going in to have regular checkups—not because they're hypochondriacs but because it makes sense.

Honey, I know you're sick, but you're making *me* sick!

Sweetie, you are driving me nuts with your endless demands. You don't have cancer. You have the flu. I know it's a bona fide illness. I know you're uncomfortable. I know it's a hassle. And I do love you and want to care for you. But I'm asking you to show just a little appreciation for the fact that I'm trying to tend to your needs in addition to my full load of regular responsibilities. Instead, I feel like I'm being ordered around as if I were a hired nurse.

I'm tending you out of love. Show me a little love in return. A few less complaints. A few less demands. And a little more acknowledgment that your being sick does not mean I can just put everything else in my life on hold and be with you full time.

You and I need to talk. To someone professional.

We're not communicating. We seem to relate to each other's way of thinking like two medieval knights clanging broadswords upon armour—an arduous, pointless, frustrating, and ultimately absurd thing to do.

We need someone to help us get out of our armour and stop fighting. Nobody's winning here. We need a referee.

Let's get some therapy.

If we really want to get on with this relationship it's the thing to do.

I don't want our next vacation spoiled by things we feel obliged to do.

I'm thinking about our next vacation and I don't want it to be like the last one. Here's a list of things I'm tired of pretending I enjoy:

- Museums. I have nothing against museums. We have museums right here within driving distance that we never even *think* about visiting in the normal course of everyday life. So why should the prospect of yet another museum to visit on my vacation magically turn me on?

- Churches, cathedrals, monuments, cemeteries, the houses where famous people lived, squares, ruins, the sites of famous events: ditto.

- Pictures. We hardly ever take a snapshot of anything at home. Yet when we go away, we bring twenty-five rolls of film like we were on assignment for *The National Geographic*. I feel like we've seen whole places solely through a camera viewfinder. Developing the film costs a fortune. And most of the stuff we take doesn't even come out.

- Postcards. When we go somewhere supposedly to relax, I feel like we spend at least a quarter of the time worrying about postcards, looking for postcards, filling out postcards: writing, writing, writing until my fingers cramp. If I really wanted to do all that writing, I'd take a writing course, not a vacation.

- Souvenirs. God, the junk we buy and lug home and force upon our friends and relatives who don't really want it. On our next vacation, no matter where we go, let's just plead insanity to everyone, not send a million postcards, spend a mint on native junk that people only accept out of politeness, or take a million pictures that we have to force people to look at. Let's forget museums and cathedrals and ruins and such. Let's just relax and be with each other in the fresh change of scenery we both really need.

And whether or not we scale a Rocky or an Alp just because it's there—let's just make those decisions jointly day by day.

I don't know about you, but I need a *real* day off.

This Saturday, let's not do any chores. None! No cooking, no cleaning, no paying the bills, no mowing the lawn, nothing! It won't be a major catastrophe if the house is left untouched for a few days or if we have to shop for groceries a little earlier than usual or if the weeds in the garden are allowed to grow for another week.

And even if it is a big deal, so what?

I need a day when I can get out of bed anytime I want—at noon if it works out that way. We spend each weekend creating more work for ourselves instead of using that time off from "regular" work for what it was intended: leisure!

So . . . at the end of this week, forget stripping the paint off old furniture. Cross recaulking the windows off our list of things we have to do. Cancel all time-consuming projects that are just plain not fun.

Let's declare next weekend our Non-Labor Days, and celebrate by giving ourselves a real rest. Let's just goof off. It will give us a chance to recharge our batteries and plunge back into the business of life with fresh energy next week.

VIII

PEOPLE

What is there to say about people? Plenty! You hate them. You love them. They're the source of your greatest joys—and perhaps your greatest miseries, too. These articulations help you address how you and your man get along with all kinds of people: the ones in his life, the ones in yours, the ones you tend to spend time with together—friends, siblings, parents, co-workers. But in here you'll also find conversation starters on people *issues*. How you and your man interact with people as a couple. Renewing friendships you've allowed to lapse. And dealing with the problem of people you don't like—yet sometimes can't avoid.

Do your friends like me?

I'm concerned that your friends don't like me. I know they go through the motions of being polite, and yet there's a kind of relaxed way all of you interrelate that I don't feel a part of. When someone asks me a question, I get the sense that it's a deliberate effort to include me. It just feels a little forced. And when I pick that up, it makes me self-conscious, as if I don't quite fit in.

Or when I answer that person, sometimes there's just a split second of hesitation, and then everybody kind of jumps in at once, with a flurry of phrases like "Oh, sorry" and "No, you go first"—to see who'll actually deal with what I said. It just makes me feel uncomfortable, as if I said something the group as a whole, because they think the same way, collectively finds strange.

The result is I feel out of it even more.

Can you understand why I feel a little insecure around them? You mean so much to me. I want so much to fit into your life— including your social life. I really *want* your friends to like me, not just because I'm your partner but in my own right. Because if they only like me as your partner, then they're really just sort of *tolerating* me. They're not genuinely liking me because I'm *me*.

I know being liked that way takes time. But do you think they ever will?

My friends can't believe that two people as different as we are can have a real relationship.

My friends really like you, but they also feel a little awkward around you. And I must admit, it makes me smile. You're not like any other guy I've introduced to them.

But from their more objective and detached point of view, the men I've gone out with in the past were quite similar to me. We had the same sort of backgrounds. We had the same sensibilities. We had exactly the same tastes in everything: food, movies, music—you name it. We reacted to the same things in the same ways.

It got so my friends could predict the type of guy I'd end up with. And now, because you are who you are, they have to revise the way they think about *me,* which they never expected to have to do.

I just wanted you to know that, in case you were picking up any funny vibes around them. If you are, it's only them adjusting to you. Because, even though they think you're neat, they also say wonderingly, and maybe just a tad enviously, "But I can't get over how *different* he is from you."

To which I reply: "That's why I fell for him. He's one of a kind."

The people you work with seem cut from the same cloth: burlap.

I'm sure the guys at your job have their good points, but as an outsider, my perspective on them may be somewhat different from yours.

To me, they're like men from another age: the Stone Age.

They get their jollies by telling ethnic jokes. Haw, haw.

They talk with their mouths full. Yuck.

They use locker-room language that makes even me want to blush. Or vanish. Or explode. Or barf.

Their two favorite subjects are sports and the weather. *Bor-ing.*

And when one of them pats me on the behind like it was some sort of public good-luck piece, I want to haul off and drop-kick him into the middle of next week.

As far as I'm concerned, their sole virtue is the fact that *you* seem to like them or at least hang around with them some of the time, and since I'm the woman in your life, I suppose it's my curse to bear that burden, too.

Up to a point.

But now that you know how I really feel, would you save my appearance for some really important occasion, and just tell them I'm a sickly sort, or whatever you think they'll buy the rest of the time to explain my absence.

In theory, I'd like to be one of the guys. But your guys just keep reminding me that I'm a member of the opposite sex.

The people at my job are starting to play guessing games about what you're like.

When I tell them you're not the Invisible Man, they laugh and tease me, because we've been together for a while and they still haven't even seen you, let alone socialized with you.

Would you humor all of us and stop by the office sometime soon just to say hi to everyone? It doesn't have to be a major production. Pick me up one day next week after work. The girls just want to get a peek at you so they will have something else to gossip about. And the guys who might have wanted to take me out are dying to know what kind of man I've chosen so that I'm "unavailable."

Come on. Aren't you a little bit flattered that they're curious about you? Indulge us. Let me show you off.

When I see you kiss another woman on the cheek, my heart skips a beat.

What is it about your women friends that makes it so easy for you to talk to them when you and I often have trouble communicating?

I know some of your former girlfriends have become "just friends," but how do I know they're going to stay that way?

When you flirt with your women friends and give them a hug or a kiss, I know I shouldn't feel jealous or threatened, but I do. Even though you've told me a million times that I'm the only girl for you, when I see you with your women friends, no matter what the relationship is, was, or will be, I feel insecure. I can't help it.

It's not only that I'm envious of the way you act with them, the ease with which you all interrelate, it's also that I wish you'd only act that way with me. I know that's unrealistic. I guess I just need some reassurance from you. The women who are your friends are valuable for you to have. I understand. I think they're "good people," too. I do.

But I don't think I'll ever be totally comfortable around them until I learn to overcome this feeling of jealousy and insecurity I have, no matter how unfounded it is.

Can you help me do that, or is it something I have to do alone?

I wish you wouldn't treat my guy friends like the competition.

You don't have any competition. You're my man. Believe it. It's true. Please don't act so territorial and possessive around guys who've been my friends for years. They're like my big brothers. They care for me just like they'd care for a little sister. Before I met you, they looked out for me. They protected me. They helped me out when I needed help. You and I might never have met were it not for them. I'm not saying that they actually saved my life, but they *influenced* my life, helped give it shape and direction, and ultimately the path I took led to you.

You may think I flirt with them but we're really just kidding around. It's just a sign of how comfortable we feel around each other based on years of caring and affection in the best, most innocent, most wholesome sense. Even though I know I now have you to look out for me, I could count on them as friends to protect me if you weren't around. I wish you'd feel more secure just knowing that there are people in this world I could turn to if I really needed help and you weren't able to give it to me.

If you'd just not let your imagination run wild, and try to know them better and watch how we interact, you'd realize that they're not out to make a conquest. They're just good friends. They want the best for me. And as such, they're interested in you, too. That's why they feel safe flirting with me when you're around. It's so obvious they assume you understand we're all just old friends.

If your boss and you aren't related, why do I feel like he's a member of the family?

Every day when you come home from work it's: "My boss made me do this. My boss said that. Do you know what that bastard did? Do you know what he thinks? Can you guess what he's going to do next? Can you intuit the logic underlying this action?"—or that deed, or some misdeed, or some cardinal corporate sin, or some crime against humanity?

God, I'm so sick of hearing about your boss! Your boss is worse than a mother-in-law. I feel like I should set a place for him at the dinner table. He's the talk of every meal. You know, *I* have a boss, too. Why can't we talk about *my* boss once in a while? How come your boss gets all the airtime around here? Isn't there anything else we can talk about—some nonwork-related things? I realize that nothing else in life can compare to this near-demonic presence in your life, but can't you tear your mind away from this guy for five minutes?

When we're socializing as a couple, you can turn from Dr. Jekyll into Mr. Hyde.

When we're alone together at home you're fine. You're polite and fairly considerate and we don't seem to have much problem conducting civilized conversations.

But when we're out together in public, it's like this whole other side of you comes out. You ignore what I say when we're talking to someone else. Or you dismiss me by snapping, "Don't mind her." Or you turn to me and say, "Will you shut up!" Not only do you shock and embarrass me, but you should see the looks your behavior elicits from other people. They are positively appalled!

Don't ever speak to me that way again, do you hear? I don't like it. I won't tolerate it. It's not fair. It's not right. I'm not going to put up with it anymore.

If you're ashamed of me, then let's break up. But if you love me, I expect you to act like it in public, in private, in a taxi, on a plane, in a movie theater: *everywhere!*

Don't you treat me like a child. I'm not a child. Don't you treat me like some half-wit. Especially in front of other people. I've got as much brains as you do and I want you to show your respect for that fact all the time.

If you can't handle that, if you have a problem with that, if you don't like the sound of that, I want to know it right now.

Guess who my favorite people aren't?

If you don't know who I don't like, I'll give you some hints.

I don't like men who treat me like "the little woman." I am an adult, and your equal.

I don't like women who look me up and down like vultures sizing up their prey. I'm not competing with them for your attention. If they think we're in some sort of contest with you as the prize, that's their problem.

I don't like people who at parties split into two groups: The women go off into one corner of the room for "girl talk" while the men break out the brandy and cigars to discuss affairs of state. I'm not an airhead. I can talk about politics or money or sports as well as anyone else.

I don't like people who patronize me or treat me condescendingly or think they're better than I am or who are just plain snobs.

You know the type of people I mean. At least I think you do. If you're still not sure, I'll be glad to tell you, because I don't want to be around them any more than I have to, if I have to at all.

Being in love doesn't mean we have to tell our friends, "Sorry."

Sweetie, I know you prefer my company to everyone else's, and I love you for it, but no couple is an island. Our friends haven't heard from us in ages. I suspect they're starting to think we don't like them anymore.

Can you remember the last time we had anyone over? Can you recall when we ourselves went out visiting? It's been *that* long!

We're becoming couch potatoes! I think that's fine once in a while, but we shouldn't let it become chronic. We've invested too much time in building friendships with some really nice people to let those relationships die of neglect. We can't just call folks from out of the blue after months of silence and expect them to fall all over themselves because we deigned to communicate. If we ignore people for too long, it's natural for them to think they're not important to us. We have to make an effort to show them they're wrong.

Let's put ourselves back into circulation. If we get some stimulation from the outside world, we'll be better companions for each other. We know single people who are dating. We know couples who are considering marriage. We know married people who are debating whether or not to have kids. We know parents whose children are growing up—fast. And a lot has happened with us, too.

We've *all* got a lot of catching up to do. I'm not saying we have to throw a major party but why can't we call someone up and ask if they want to get together—even if it's just for drinks?

IX

FAMILY LIFE

Here are some articulations on touchy subjects—getting married, getting separated, having children, getting along with your parents, and clarifying your responsibilities to your family, to name just a few. The interactions among people in the course of family living can often be frustrating and bewildering, but this chapter will help you ease the stress of being unable to say what you feel about family matters of all sorts.

I think about marriage all the time.

I grew up believing I'd be married one day and begin a family of my own. I assumed it was my destiny and I looked forward to it. I just took for granted that things would naturally fall into place.

But I'm past the age when I dreamed I'd be married. And I see single women even younger than me who are already starting to look desperate, without a life partner and afraid they'll be alone forever. I read articles about a woman's dwindling chances of finding a husband, and I find it impossible to keep on pretending that the general concern hasn't touched me. It has.

You and I have been with each other for a while now. We passed the stage where we thought of ourselves as "just dating" a long time ago. We keep saying we love each other. We're living almost as if we're married—almost, but not quite. But to me, the difference between *almost* being married and *being* married is getting bigger every day.

I love you. You say you love me. I'm asking you now to prove you really mean it. Let's make our relationship official. Let's become husband and wife.

It could be I'm falling out of love.

Once I thought I loved you. Now I'm not so sure. Yes, we've changed over time, but that's only part of it. In some ways we haven't changed, and I guess I assumed one of us or both of us would.

I feel confused. I don't know *what* I feel. One minute I say to myself, "Stick it out. Make it work. Don't be a quitter." And I feel guilty. But then I think, "Look, he's not a bad person. But here's his set of needs. Here's yours. And they're just not the same any more. No one's to blame. But the relationship's stopped working for you. You can do something about it or you can go on suffering in silence."

Well, I don't want to suffer in silence. I want to do something, something that's in my power to do. It's not in my power to change you. *That* much I've learned. So I'm giving some serious thought to the only alternative left that I can think of: a trial separation.

If you have another suggestion, I'd like to hear it.

You'd probably prefer it if I were an orphan.

But I'm not.

You don't like my parents. Okay, I'd rather it was otherwise, but that's the way things are.

That doesn't excuse you from having to spend any time with them or from being nice to them when you do.

Even if my father always tells you the same stories, or my mother tries to get me into a conversation that seems to exclude you purposely, try to remember that I'm their daughter and they care about me. Don't put me into an uncomfortable situation by acting distant and displeased when we're with my folks. Your attitudes and behavior make you look bad to them, and even if you don't care what they think about you, I'm the one who gets to listen to them put you down, and they do complain to me about you.

It's a drag to be in the middle, getting flak from you about them and the same from them about you. I love you and I tell them that, even if the way you act makes them wonder what it is about you that appeals to me. So I tell them you're wonderful and I'm telling you now, my parents are good people, too.

Put yourself in my shoes. If you try to make the best of this situation, it'll probably take care of itself.

Your parents make it clear I'm not the girl for you, and I'm still waiting for you to object.

Apparently your mother and father had some vision of the perfect woman for you and somehow I don't fill the bill. Well, I don't like that, but I can live with it.

But I *am* supposed to be *your* vision of the perfect woman for you, and when your parents get on my case, and you let them, as if you were unaware of their opprobrium toward me, or worse: as if it were okay—that I *can't* live with.

When your parents belittle me, when they say unflattering things, when they criticize me, when they treat me coldly, when everything about their expressions, their manner, their tones of voice, and the things they say only serve to show their continued and intensifying disdain for me, I expect you to put your foot down and speak up in my behalf.

I can defend myself, thank you, but since it's your parents and I'm doing my best to be courteous and civil, which is more than they're doing, I shouldn't have to tell you to step in there and intercede.

You should say without prompting, "Mom, Dad, give this woman a break. She may not be what you had in mind for me, but it's my life and I love her a lot, so lay off, okay?"

Because if you really loved me, you'd identify with the sense of rejection they bend over backwards to make sure I feel, and it would hurt you just as much as it hurts me, because being in love is supposed to sensitize you that way, and you'd tell them just that: "If you hurt her, you're hurting me." They'll hear that from you. They won't hear anything from me.

It's hard to believe you and your brother have the same parents.

One of you must have been stolen by gypsies—him! Or raised by wolves! His values and style are so different from yours it's like night and day.

It seems that I can't talk about anything with him without getting into—well, we don't have arguments, we just get extremely tense around each other and tight-lipped.

It's difficult for me to be around your brother. I try. I'll keep on trying. But it's tough. Can you spend some time with him without me? Maybe he feels as though I'm taking something away from him, the brother he wants and needs. Perhaps if you two just spent some time alone together, and talked about me, I bet you could make him see that I'm not a threat. He hasn't lost a brother and he'd be gaining a friend. But he has to make an effort, too.

My sister and you may not see eye to eye, but I love you both.

My sister is a very opinionated woman. She likes to be the center of attention. It can be annoying, I know.

But she's loyal and sweet and she cares about me a whole lot. Maybe too much.

There are worse things.

Okay, maybe she sends out signals that you aren't her favorite person. She has different taste from me when it comes to men, it's true.

But she watches out for me because she loves me. She's been hurt by a couple of guys and she wants to spare me the pain of what happened to her. That isn't a capital crime. And she's smart enough to realize that if I care this much about you, you must be worth caring about. Try to understand and give her a chance.

My sister is a tough cookie, but I'd trust her with my life. Since you're a part of my life, she's beginning to become aware of what you mean to me—and ultimately to her. Be patient. She'll come around. One day you'll be great friends.

Relating to your family can wear me out.

You're close to your family. Fine. My family is not so close. It's just the way things worked out. But we spend so much time with your relatives—time that I'm not accustomed to spending with my own family—that it's starting to make me feel frazzled. All this intense family socializing is a drain. I need a break from it.

Please don't take this as criticism. I'm not knocking your relatives. I was just brought up differently and I'm used to a different way of interacting with the people in my family, one that isn't so formalized—with command performances and everyone seemingly assigned a certain role to play.

I didn't fully appreciate when I fell in love with you how important a place your family had in your life. But now I've got an important place, too, haven't I? What I'm asking is that you try to compromise a little. I don't mind spending some time with your family. But all this relentless relating is overwhelming me. I could use a rest.

I know your mom has always come first, but now I want equal time.

It's time to take the word "always" out of your thinking regarding your mother. I understand and appreciate that she's the woman who raised you, that you love her and owe her. And I think it's great that you feel this way about your mother.

But when you and I have made plans, and then what your mother wants to do interferes, I would like you to say, "Mom, I'm sorry. We're busy at that time."

I'm not insisting that my needs should always come before your mother's, any more than I'm suggesting the reverse. But if you can never tell her no, if you always put her first, then you're not really having a relationship with me. I'm just a stand-in. You'd only have room for one woman in your life: her.

Is that the truth? Because if it isn't, you need to start telling your mother, "Not now, later," at least some of the time.

We don't have to wait for a holiday to visit our folks.

It will be easier on us if we make an effort to visit them more than once or twice a year in intense doses. Frequent short visits will mean more to them than one long, tension-filled, and argumentative week over Easter or Christmas and New Year's.

Don't you think they'd appreciate seeing us more often? I do. We may actually get to the point where we and the folks learn to enjoy each other simply because the time we'd have to interact would be short, sweet, and less of a strain.

Maybe then we won't get booked into special appearances when everyone has unrealistic expectations because of the anticipation and emotional investment riding on those infrequent visits.

And, if we visited your parents and mine more often at other times of the year, we could go skiing at Christmas or take a spring break or somehow play with the calendar with time we'd have free. Think about it.

Do we have to go home for the holidays every single year?

Boy, you know, it isn't as though we get a whole lot of time off from work as it is. And both our jobs are so demanding. They take a lot out of us. How many times do we even find ourselves working evenings and weekends, or worrying about work, which amounts to the same thing?

To me, knowing we have traditional and national holidays coming up—time we can take off without guilt because it's time off for everyone—gives me a real psychological boost.

But then we have these visits: to your parents, to my parents, to other relatives. Once in a while, they're fine. But every year? Why, they become more like duty visits—not trips one wants to make but trips one feels an obligation to make.

Even that I don't mind so much. But not always at a time when I—when most people, I think—need a break from the routine of everyday life.

Let's do something else this year. Let's unwind and relax and do only what *we* want to do. We'll call everybody and arrange some other time to visit. It's not as if we won't see them. We just won't see them at the usual time. Let's recognize that it's time we need for ourselves.

I need a vacation from family life.

This family has got more crises than a TV soap opera. It's a plot twist a minute around here. Mothers. Fathers. Sisters. Brothers. Grandparents. Cousins. Aunts. Uncles.

How can *everybody* be in a dilemma of epic proportions all at the same time? Can this be real life? It's tough to tell. The only difference between us and the tube is that they've got commercial breaks, and our lives continue with no interruptions.

If I have to handle one more catastrophe, one more issue, one more demand, I'm gonna go batty. I need a change of scenery right away. Is there such a thing as an emergency vacation? If so, I want one. If not, we have to invent one.

Let me put this as gently, as delicately, as diplomatically as I know how:

HEEEEEEEEEEEEEEELLLLLLLLLLLLLLPPPPPPPPPPPPPPP!!!

Get me out of this madhouse before I pass the point of no return.

Get the hint?

We've talked *around* having a baby. Let's talk *about* it.

Lately I've found myself looking at other people's babies and feeling a pang of longing, a sense of incompleteness, maybe even a little jealousy.

I can picture the future. It seems so clear to me: you, me, and a baby who's a combination of *us* and who represents our love, our lives, what we're creating together. It feels so *right* that there are times when I'm a bit startled that it hasn't actually happened yet.

It's time. Let's stop using contraception when we make love, okay? I feel really ready to get pregnant. Don't you want this, too?

I don't need to have children to feel complete.

I like my life the way it is. No, it's not perfect, but it's pretty good. I've got a good career. I've got a great guy. We've got our friends. We've got our families. We've got the little puttering-around sorts of things we do to relax and unwind. We take a vacation now and then, which we always need and always feels like it's long past due.

How much can a person cram into one life? No more than that. We're all up against the immutable fact of the twenty-four-hour day. We all need to eat and sleep. Part of me would like to have a child—if I didn't have to give up a life that I've constructed piece by piece to work for me. But I would. I could never be a half-baked mother, and I really wouldn't even have time to be that if I didn't make some other major sacrifice: my work, our friends—something, not to mention my sense of personal satisfaction and emotional well-being.

I know you say you'd help out with a baby, but that's just it: You would *only* help. You and I both know who would bear the lion's share of responsibility for child rearing. I'd like it if—but there are always ifs attached to things we don't really want. Motherhood isn't for me. We're talking about an eighteen-year commitment. It's nearly impossible to imagine if you think of it that way. And that *is* how I think of it: Instead of my career, it would have to become my big focus in life. Our relationship would suffer. Our friendships would suffer. My career, my dreams—I could kiss them goodbye.

No, thank you. I'm one of the few people I know who *likes* her life. I feel more complete now than I'd ever thought possible. Why would I want to give that up?

146

We can't have a child on our own. What are we going to do about it?

We could cry, curse our fate, and try to forget about it. Act of God. That sort of thing. Or we could do something more hopeful.

We could try to adopt. Years of red tape. Major hassle. Still no guarantees. But it's an alternative.

We could try something modern. Artificial insemination. In vitro fertilization. Surrogate mother. There are new medical possibilities every day. I know it's not traditional, but at least it's an alternative open to us.

The point is we talked about having a baby and agreed we wanted one. I didn't get pregnant. The doctors have told us why. But we haven't had a real discussion since then about how we feel. Can we do that now?

Maybe I'm not ready to have a baby.

Am I? Aren't I? I keep vacillating back and forth. I'm getting worn out just trying to make up my mind.

How would it affect my career? Or is that being selfish? Would I make a good mother? Or is that just a dumb question? Will I still be glad to have a child during the terrible twos and threes and tens, or is talk like that irresponsible?

I don't know. I think I ought to feel a little more sure of myself before we decide to take this big step. I mean, part of me wants to do it now. But our lives would change so much—the time, the money, the concern, the physical and emotional energy, the sheer fatigue of it all—when I think about all that, I find myself hesitant, thinking, "Hey, wait a minute. Are you really ready to go the whole nine yards? Because if you're not, it would be a bad idea to bring a child into this world—bad for you, for the baby, for all of us."

Then I find myself mired down by indecision again. Perhaps we should just wait a few months or a year and see if my reservations seesaw more one way than the other. It may be that this just isn't the right move for me at this time of life—or maybe ever.

X

WORK

Work for women has changed with dramatic speed. Men, as a result, have had to learn to cope with all sorts of new nuances of togetherness. They've had to adjust to a world of working women. The catch is that it's women who are usually raised to accommodate change—and even you may be finding the world you live in today much different from the one you thought you would enter when you grew up. In his own way, your man may feel just as taxed in trying to comprehend a whole new set of unwritten rules. These articulations will help. They focus on work issues that may cause tension in your relationship—workaholism, whose job is more important, getting fired, getting promoted—that most couples experience continually during their professional lives. Here is a chapter you can turn to again and again to seek new insights.

Can we talk about something other than work?

If I complain to you one more time about my job my brain will turn to Jell-O.

If I have to listen to you recount the intricacies of your work again I'm going to hurl myself out of the window.

Can't we talk about the philosophy of Hegel, plasma physics, or the school of economics of Adam Smith—something light and uncomplicated and nonwork-related for a change?

I realize it's hard for both of us to believe, but there are one or two more interesting things in life other than our careers.

How I long to go to sleep at night and have a horrible nightmare about unresolved oedipal conflicts, or even little men from outer space kidnapping me. Instead, I just dream about work. When I wake up the next morning I feel like I just put in another eight hours on the job.

Enough!

Do you think South Korea, with its autocratic proto-democracy, will ever get together with the Soviet-backed dynastic dictatorship in the north?

I'm sorry you got fired, but it didn't happen yesterday.

I know you don't want to hear this now, but I have to tell you what our financial situation is.

We've already paid one stack of bills out of our savings. Another stack of bills is coming up. The money we've got in the bank is shrinking. Fast.

I understand that you feel awful. But I can't tell that to the phone company. The gas people don't accept that as a reason for not getting paid. The savings and loan doesn't want to hear about it. Neither do the credit-card companies.

If it were up to me, I would say, "I can see how badly you're hurting. Take all the time you need to get back on your feet." But it isn't up to me.

Please, get a grip on yourself. Take a deep breath, get on with your life, bury the pain of the past, declare your period of mourning over, and take that first step forward.

The first step is the hardest. You know that. Let me help. We'll check the Sunday classifieds together. I'll help you update your résumé. I'll even rehearse with you what to say when you go out on interviews. Come on. Let's work together as a team and turn this setback into a triumph.

I've always wanted my own business. I'm going for it.

I can't work for anybody else one more second! I'm tired of taking orders from fools and male chauvinists. I'm tired of doing dumb, boring, meaningless work. I'm an intelligent person who has something valuable to contribute, but I've been crushed in a box on an organizational chart and I'm spending the bulk of my professional life playing politics, rather than creating something worthwhile.

For a while, we'll be a one-income couple until I get this new venture on its feet, and I'm going to need your support—not just financially, but emotionally and intellectually. There are times I'll be frustrated. There are times I'll be unsure. There are times when I may feel like a failure and want to give up. That's when I'll need you to be there for me with sympathy and expert advice.

It's going to be tough on you because I'll probably be working night and day to get this business off the ground, but despite the strain this may put on our relationship temporarily, it doesn't mean that being together won't matter to me. I'll still love you and care about you, and when I find myself working long hours, I'll miss you, too.

The difference is that it'll be long hours for *my* own business, not someone else's, and that, eventually, will change me—and us—for the better.

You may have a demanding job, but you need to do more than just squeeze me in.

When we started to date, I knew you worked hard, but I didn't know you were an addict. How could I? You managed to find time—enough time—to spend with me so that I felt something substantial was binding us together.

Your ambition is one of the things that attracted me to you. And I've never begrudged you the hours you put in on the job. I've always felt that it was more important that our time together be quality time, not quantity time.

But the time we spend together now is neither quality nor quantity. We don't seem to spend much time together at all. Lately I feel like I mainly see you just before you hit the sack half-dead with exhaustion at night, and for a moment or two when the alarm goes off in the morning.

I'm afraid I bargained for more in a relationship than that. I have no idea what you expect me to do while you spend more hours per day for a greater and greater block of days doing nothing but work. The way things stand now, if I found someone else and simply left you, I think it would be weeks before you'd even noticed.

If work really means that much to you, I know I can't fight it. I'll leave you to it. I'll leave you—period. Because what I've got now is worse than being alone. Is that what you want? If not, you need to refocus some of that work energy right here, right now: on me, on us, on our relationship—what's left of it.

If you were offered a great job in another part of the country, would you ask me before you said yes?

I guess what I'm asking is how important I am to you, and if you would not assume that my job and friends, my attachments and obligations, come second in this relationship. I'd like to know that you would consult me if you were offered even the most fantastic opportunity in a strange place, and not act as if it were a given that I would drop my life here and blindly follow you.

I might follow you simply because I love you. But I don't know if I would do it without being given the opportunity to decide. And I'd want to see how you would feel if I decided *not* to go with you because my roots are here. Would a geographical career move be as tempting to you if you knew you were leaving me behind?

I know these may not be easy questions to answer. But I'd like to know you would not take for granted that where you go, I will naturally follow.

Until I get settled at my new job, I'm probably going to be distracted, exhausted, and nervous.

It seems to be easier for you to move into a new work environment than it is for me. Maybe that's a difference between men and women, I don't know. Men seem to have this socialized sense of entitlement that makes it easier for them to relocate into strange surroundings, make themselves at home, take charge, and assume their "rightful" place in a new company.

It's different for women, I think, at least it is for me. I always feel like I'm being tested, like if I don't make a terrific first impression everyone will think, "God, what a loser."

Also, I think I have a stronger need to be liked than you do. It's important to me to be able to fit in, at least somewhat, and to get along with my coworkers, and to have us all feel comfortable working with each other.

But trying to accomplish all that *and* see to all my new professional responsibilities at the same time is a lot to be handling at once. So if you occasionally find me lost in thought, or wiped out pretty often for the next month or two, or all tensed up, please understand that—well, it goes with the territory—and eventually I'll settle down, regain my confidence, and seem more like my usual self.

The fact that I got promoted makes us both look good.

I get the impression that you feel somewhat threatened by my promotion. You've been acting a little cold toward me ever since I told you about it, or sometimes you snap at me, which you didn't do so much before, or you'll make a sarcastic comment—something to try to bring me down.

I know that it's tough to see someone move up and get a new title and get a raise when you don't, and I know that the fact that we both earn close to the same amount of money bothers you. You feel that it's somehow more masculine or a man's right to earn more, that men, after all, do a better job.

Well, they don't do a better job. Some men do a great job. But so do some women. It's time to put this sexist business behind you and think of me—professionally at least—not as a woman but just as a person for whom good, better, or best has nothing to do with gender. Because that's a lot closer to the business world as it exists today.

Besides, we're not in competition with each other. We're a couple. We're a team. I want you to feel proud of me. I want you to love the fact that I've accomplished something and now I'm getting rewarded for it. I want you to support me in doing even better next time. And I'll do the same for you. When your turn comes for a promotion and a raise, I'll be the loudest cheerleader. I won't be down in the dumps, and you wouldn't want me to be.

So be glad for me. Be glad for us! I didn't win alone. Our team won. This recognition does credit to us both.

I guess this wasn't your year.

I'm sorry you didn't get that promotion. You deserved it. I know how hard you worked to earn it. I can see how disappointed you are, and I suspect you feel like you failed somehow, even though we don't really know all the factors used to fill that job upstairs.

But we both know politics played a part in it. That's no reflection on your competence, your skills, your intelligence, your professionalism, your dedication, your drive, your sense of purpose, your knowledge, or your ability to perform. And I won't stand by and let you beat yourself up as if you weren't good enough, didn't make the grade, and now are something less than you were the moment before you learned it wasn't you who got the promotion.

It'll be your year next year. Don't get angry. Don't give up. This too shall pass.

Just because you make more money than I do doesn't mean my job is less important than yours.

Sometimes you make me feel like my contribution to our income doesn't matter. It does. What if I suddenly lost my job or I decided to quit? We've got all sorts of monthly payments to meet. If my salary suddenly stopped, we'd feel it. And we'd feel it right away.

But that's just the beginning. My job matters to me the same way yours matters to you. It's not just what I do. It's also who I am. When you make it seem like it's only money, nothing more, and then say, "Hah, I earn more than you," I feel like you judge my worth as a person on the basis of what I get paid. And I don't like that.

I may not earn megabucks but I get personal pride and satisfaction from my work and my ability to do it well. And you can't put a price tag on that. Doesn't that start to blur the distinction between who earns what?

Do you think that just because I work at home I've got time to do all your errands?

Listen, I'm running a full-fledged business here. I've got deadlines to meet, professional responsibilities, overhead, bills, invoices, cash-flow problems—the same sort of stuff every other type of businessperson has to deal with, except that I happen to work out of my home instead of an office.

But just because the washing machine happens to be in the next room that doesn't mean I have time to do your laundry during the day. It doesn't mean I can just hop in the car and pick up your clothes from the drycleaner. It doesn't mean I'm secretly having ladies' teas during the day while you're slaving away at a "regular" job.

This *is* a "regular" job! And I'm slaving away, too. It makes me furious that you think that just because I'm working at home I'm not doing "real" work and have all kinds of time to do your chores. From where I sit, you're the one who has it easy. You only have to work from nine to five. Yes, I have the freedom to set my own hours. But like most entrepreneurs, that means I usually work twice as hard, and on evenings and weekends as well. As you've seen. Please don't give me your chores to do. There aren't enough hours in my day as it is.

I'm afraid people will find out who I really am: just a little nobody.

Sometimes I feel like a complete phony in my job. I'm not what people really think I am. I'm a lot less.

Well, I guess I've had *some* accomplishments. But I don't even feel comfortable accepting compliments or congratulations for anything. I don't deserve them. Or sometimes I think maybe I do, but I can't hold onto the feeling. Or when someone says something nice to me about my work, I don't think they're really being sincere. How could they sincerely be complimenting *me?*

God, I feel so miserable. I'm successful, I suppose, and yet I feel empty, vague, at sea, adrift. I wish I could just chuck this feeling of worthlessness and accept the credit people give me as if I were truly worth it.

Do you think I'm a fraud, too?

XI

MONEY

Everyone already talks about money—usually without much concrete result. The proof is that money is usually the single greatest source of arguments in a relationship. These articulations begin to confront in a safe and rational, though sometimes impassioned, way the money matters that so often turn out to be fuses leading to emotional powder kegs. Should, for example, your financial assets be combined with your man's or be managed separately by yourself? Your man accuses you of spending too much? Is he right? Does *he* spend too much? Does the fact that he may earn more than you give him certain rights and entitlements regarding money? And what about conflicts that may arise if he *doesn't* earn more than you? Turn the page and you'll start to see how these potentially explosive subjects can be discussed in a civilized way.

I hate doing the same job as men and getting paid less for it.

Men are supposed to be so rational, logical, and objective. But what's the logic of paying women less for equal work and equal performance?

Is it that we're less intelligent?

Is it that we're less committed?

Is it that secretly we all want to get married, have babies and be taken care of by a man—so men need to be paid more to enable us to realize our dream?

Is it that we may get pregnant and need to take five minutes off from work to give birth, and the prospect of having us gone for five minutes is so mortifying that it should be offset by a lifetime of earning inequity?

Is it because women simply require less money than men? Is it because we buy diet books and try to eat less? Is that it? In the grand scheme of things, is the difference in wages intended to help us keep our figures?

Is it because women throughout history have always been paid less, so we continue to do it out of cherished tradition?

Is this something the Bible says to do? Is there an Eleventh Commandment that states, "Thou shalt pay women less"?

And if this is really an okay thing to do, how come the companies that do it keep it a secret? If they aren't ashamed, why don't they just come right out and nail it to the public bulletin board, like "his and hers" towels in the bathroom: Men earn this, women who do the same job earn that?

Do you know the answer to any of this stuff? Don't you think it would tick *you* off if the situation were reversed?

You say I spend too much. I say I don't.

I manage money quite well, thank you, despite your misperceptions.

It's true that I spend more money on clothes and makeup than you do. But if I didn't, you'd know it, and you'd be the first to complain, because how good I look is also a reflection on you.

Then there's the running of our household—a little chore that gets delegated to me by default, even though you're not the only one around here who puts in long hours at a job. If I serve hot dogs for dinner, you frown at the plate and say, "What's this? Baseball food?"

Well, if you want steak, you need to spend more. Do you know how much sirloin costs per pound these days? What about flank steak? Or ribeye. Or rump roast? Or T-bone? It's your appetite that governs the amount of our food bills for the most part, not mine.

And there are other fun things to buy: toilet paper and dish detergent and plastic garbage bags and paper towels and toothpaste and Brillo—Gosh, what a gas! You're lucky I don't go hog-wild out of sheer ecstasy and double our spending on such stuff.

I don't think you realize where the money really goes, and how little things that you like and take for granted—soft toilet paper instead of the store brand, which costs a quarter less—begin to add up until collectively you get the sum that you see.

So lower your eyebrows or lower your expectations. The choice, as usual, is left up to you.

Let's treat saving money like a habit, not a chore.

Maybe saving money is so hard for us because we're taking the wrong approach to it. We always need things or at least want things, so that not buying them in order to save money for something else—something bigger and longer-term and ultimately more important—isn't very gratifying. Like doing the dishes or taking out the trash isn't very gratifying; they're just things that have to be done.

But we do them without thinking about them. And perhaps we can take that same attitude toward money we want to save. Maybe it can be like brushing our teeth. That's something we just do automatically, out of habit. Whether it's interesting or not, whether it feels good or not, isn't an issue. It just never comes up.

Let's pick a realistic amount that we can set aside from our paychecks every week and put it in the bank. And once we decide what that sum is, let's not have any more discussion about it. Let's just do it. Automatically. We can turn saving into a habit if we just make a commitment to do it and then have the discipline not to renege later on.

Having you invest both our savings is a good idea. I hope.

I know you know more about Wall Street than I do. And I know that putting money in the bank doesn't give you a whole lot of interest these days.

But this whole business of stocks and bonds and mutual funds and treasury bills and certificates of deposit and gold and futures is Greek to me. My money, though, isn't Greek to me. I know exactly what I had to do to earn it: work my tail off. And, yes, I want it to grow. And, yes, I'm willing to assume some risk to do it. And the fact is that I have confidence in your ability to wheel and deal in financial markets I know next to nothing about.

But can you appreciate how "iffy" I feel about the whole thing? I feel like I spent a few weeks in jump school learning how to parachute out of a plane and now here I am at ten thousand feet, standing before the open doorway, and what do I see at mv feet? The possibility of complete disaster.

So it just makes me a little nervous to hand my savings over to you to invest, even though I wouldn't do it if I didn't want to. I guess I just need you to reassure me yet again that I'm not making a major mistake.

Those "little" things you buy for yourself sure do add up.

Are you aware of how much money you spend during a typical month?

$50 for designer sunglasses.

$30 for a gold-plated ballpoint pen.

$65 for an alligator belt.

$25 for a bottle of wine for an ordinary restaurant lunch.

$75 for a new wallet. Hey, come on. Seventy-five bucks for a wallet? That's a lot of bread. Okay, so you don't buy a new wallet every month, or a new pen. But then it's something else. A sweater. Tickets to a ball game. Restaurant meals. Football pools. Poker night. A money clip.

Do you know you've got a wallet for your back pocket, a wallet for the breast pocket of your jacket, *and* a money clip! What you don't have is money to put into all those containers. Because all these little expenses are draining our income dry.

Would you try to be more aware before you reach for your wallet next time—whether it's the one in your pants or the one in your jacket or some new one behind the department store counter that you suddenly feel you can't live without?

Which of our necessities are really necessary?

We're living over our heads. Each month, we're barely able to pay the bills. Right now we're at the point where we may have to call our creditors and beg for extra time. I don't like that. It's humiliating and it makes us seem financially irresponsible, which is just what we've been.

We've had this discussion before. Supposedly, we pared our expenses "to the bone."

Obviously, *that* hasn't worked.

We need a new definition of what "to the bone" means. We need to take one more long hard look at our spending habits and make some new, personal policy decisions about what's really necessary for our financial survival and what we—in a worst-case scenario—could do without if there were no other choice.

After all, what are our *true* necessities, without any ifs, ands or buts?

Housing.

Food. (And we could significantly cut down the cost of that.)

The telephone. (Minus most of our expensive, long-distance calls.)

Utilities. (Minus air conditioning in the summer. If it comes down to it, we could get a cheap fan and make do.)

Credit-card payments. (Without charging anything else.)

And that is *it!*

If we add up the cost of just those things, and subtract it from what we both earn, *then* we can decide what we can't live without based on what's left.

Just because I've agreed to combine our incomes it doesn't mean you get to dole out my spending money.

Something I didn't plan on is happening with us financially. I thought we agreed to combine our incomes because it would double our spending power and saving power as a couple. But I never intended my agreement to do that to suggest that I wanted to abdicate my decision-making responsibilities concerning what I need to spend myself to get through a typical week.

I feel like you're giving me an allowance, like you're the parent and I'm the child, and I don't like that one bit. Just because you're the man around here it doesn't mean you're the superior. We're equal partners in this relationship, aren't we—*especially* when it comes to money?

We need to sit down and work out a new arrangement for personal expenses in which we both agree to how much each of us gets, not with you just handing me a few bucks and saying, "Here's some money for you."

If that's the way it's going to be, maybe we should talk about separating our assets again.

Nothing personal, but I can handle my own money, thank you.

I've worked hard to get to this point where I can be financially independent, and I don't want to give that up. It's important to me.

I realize there are some advantages to combining our earning clout, and maybe one day I'll take you up on your offer to pool our cash and other assets, but right now I want that piece of our lives to stay separate and distinct.

You pride yourself on your independence in plenty of ways. Money happens to be one of them. Maybe traditionally women were usually dependent on men for money, but all that's in the past. I thought one of the things that attracted you to me was the fact that I'm a successful and accomplished career woman who wouldn't need to depend on you. If this is a hint that you want a more traditional kind of relationship, I have no choice but to tell you you've picked the wrong woman.

It's my brains and my sweat that earns me my paycheck and I want it to stay in my wallet and in my bank. I want my checks to have my name on them, get advice from my money manager, and see my accountant at tax time. I don't pressure you to let me handle your financial affairs. Don't pressure me.

Let's try life without credit cards.

This may be the most astonishing, shocking, and flabbergasting thing you've ever heard, but I'm going to say it anyway and I want you to give it some serious thought.

We're credit-card addicts. We see something we want and it's just so easy to reach for the plastic and presto: instant gratification.

But our monthly installments are really starting to get out of hand. After we've paid our survival expenses, just about everything else goes into this black hole of debt we've built up from handing our little rectangles of plastic to one salesperson after another.

Enough!

The interest alone is killing us! Eighteen percent here. Twenty percent there! Month after month. Half the time all we do is pay off the interest and don't even make a dent in the principal. It's got to stop before we get ourselves into hot water.

Let's just take the credit cards out of our wallets and put them in a dresser drawer. Better yet, let's put them in a safe-deposit box in a bank vault where it won't be so easy for anyone to get at them—including us.

I want to know how much money we have.

Are you fooling around with our finances or something? What is this big secret about the sum total of what we're worth? Is this some male thing that nobody's allowed to know? What do you think I'm going to do: tell the world? Nag you to spend it on me? Treat you differently in any way?

It's hard enough to trust each other enough to let down our guards so that we can be intimate with each other about feelings, about sex, about love—about far more difficult topics than money. But if you insist on keeping me in the dark about that, it's as if you're telling me you're incapable of being intimate with me about things that are really important to our relationship.

All I'm asking for is one simple fact. We've supposedly made a commitment to each other. We're a couple. Why can't I know what we as a couple are worth?

XII

POWER

Do you feel absolutely equal to your man in terms of power? Of course not. In some areas of life, you're the one who has the clout. In others, he has the power. But power isn't something that's graven in stone. Power in a relationship is a commodity. It can be shared or not, effective or frustrated, put to constructive use or abused. The constructive use of power is what these articulations will help you discuss. Who gets to make the big decisions—and why? Does your man expect you to be at his beck and call? What if the balance of power in your relationship is suddenly interrupted—suppose, for example, your man loses his job? And what if he thinks up front or deep-down that women are really the weaker sex? Here are ways to start talking about how you can make power work for you as a couple instead of pull you apart.

Why do you always get to make the big decisions?

Look, I don't want to be *the* decision maker around here. And I'm not criticizing the decisions you make. But I'm an equal partner in this relationship, and I want an equal say in what we as a couple decide to do. Especially when it's a big decision involving a lot of money or a major life change.

That's the advantage of *being* a couple: having a partner to share your concerns with and discuss the pros and cons of a big decision—knowing that the other person loves you and cares as much as you do about the outcome.

Can't we collaborate as members of the same team? Because if we're *not* that, I'd like to know what you think we are.

If you want me to call the shots, you have to accept the decisions I make.

Somehow, I got delegated the responsibilities for maintaining this relationship. Making our social plans. Paying the bills. Buying the things we regularly need. Balancing the checkbook. These aren't things I wanted to do. But they weren't getting done, someone had to do them, and I just moved in to fill the gap.

But when you criticize how I do this stuff, it makes me angry. I don't get a kick out of paying the bills. It's boring. If you want to pay them, fine. I'd love it. But if you say to me, either explicitly or implicitly, "No, you do it," I don't want to hear afterward, "How come you paid the phone bill this month when you know they'll wait and we could have used the money someplace else?" Or just the opposite, like, "Why did you only pay the minimum amount due on the credit card when they're charging us nearly twenty percent interest?"

It's a no-win situation. So I'm appealing to your spirit of fair play. Either live with the decisions I make, or make them yourself—which is okay by me—or we can make them together somehow. But if you don't want to be bothered with the periodic, regular responsibility of running our lives and keeping some semblance of order around here, then you forfeit the right to play armchair quarterback, too.

Otherwise, get ready to receive a handoff.

You may be bigger than I am but it doesn't make you right.

When one of our discussions becomes an argument and then that argument gets heated, you start to get very intense. Your eyes flash. Your face gets red. You hiss or scream your words.

You switch from trying to be reasonable to posing a sense of physical threat.

And if I don't say at that point, "You're right," you stand up if you're not already standing to emphasize your height, puff out your chest, open and close your hands into fists, throw up your arms, smack a fist into the palm of your hand, poke a finger at me—you act like a bully.

You try to intimidate me with the fact that, if it came down to it, you could beat me up and win an argument that way. Although I guarantee the first one would be the last.

Look, I'm not saying I'm right about every disagreement we have. But if you need to use your size, your muscle, and your maleness to convince me of the power of your ideas, it'll never work.

Because the power of persuasion is one thing. Physical power is another. I don't think you'd ever hit me, but sometimes I'm not sure. Be more aware of the way you act. I don't want to feel threatened by you. I'm surprised you ever take that tack with me. I thought you were stronger than that.

I'm beat. Why don't you run things for a while?

My brains are fried. I'm so tired I can't think straight. I just want to vegetate for a while.

Will you do me a favor?

Will you let me cry on your shoulder? Will you listen to me complain without interrupting, just because I need to give voice to my feelings? Will you pick up my household responsibilities in addition to your own for a while?

I'm making an official declaration: I'm a zombie. I just want to go to my grave and be dead until the next full moon, when I'm doomed to rise and walk the earth again.

I'm getting bent out of shape.

Rumor has it that women are more flexible than men.

Perhaps.

But you want me to be more elastic than a rubber band! No matter how resilient I try to be in accommodating your needs, following your directions, obeying your orders, and otherwise cowtowing to you, you're never satisfied.

When you come home and say, "I feel like going out for dinner tonight," and I've just spent three hours shopping and cooking, it upsets me.

When I have to give some excuse for why we're not keeping a social invitation we accepted weeks before, because at the last minute, *you're* not in the mood, it makes me angry. I might want to go—with my man at my side. And people aren't fooled by my excuses, no matter how good they are. Pretty soon we won't be invited anywhere because we can't be depended on to show up when we say we will.

Why should I have to rearrange my schedule and everyone else's? Why can't you start being more aware that other people around you have legitimate needs? I resent it when you expect me to adapt to you.

I never thought making more money than you would make me uncomfortable.

When I got that raise, you had mixed feelings about it. I could tell. I knew that you were glad for me and proud of me. But I was now earning more than you and that wasn't the way you thought life was supposed to be.

I want you to know it makes me uncomfortable, too.

For all my assertions of women's equality, which I absolutely believe intellectually, emotionally I feel a little unsettled, as if some known, traditional, accepted balance had suddenly, unwittingly been upset.

For example, when we go out to a restaurant, even though the waiter may put the check in the middle of the table between us, you're the one who picks it up. You do it automatically. I don't question it. It's not one of those things we think about.

Why not?

Because you're the man. Paying for things seems to be a basic masculine trait. But now I'm going to start paying for things as well. And even though it will make us feel a little self-conscious at first, we'll adapt to this new state of affairs.

If you want to talk about how these changes make you feel, it's a discussion I'd be glad to have. I've got plenty of adjusting to do, too. Happy as I am to have gotten a raise, I don't want it to come between us.

I want this relationship to be a democracy, not a dictatorship.

Stop giving me orders. You're not my ruler and I'm not your subject. I'm your partner in this relationship—your *equal* partner. Start acting like you understand, appreciate, and respect it.

Instead of telling me what to do all the time, ask me what I think. Invite me to sit down and discuss with you whatever is on your mind. Listen to what I have to say as if you were hearing it from another man—if that's what it takes to have you take me seriously—because when I respond to you it's a serious response.

You're not the only one around here with feelings and needs and joys and sorrows. I feel all that, too. Try sharing a little more instead of issuing commands. I don't like being ordered around. Do you like being ordered around? I doubt it.

Stop it.

That's an order!

There, how does it feel when the shoe's on the other foot?

If you think I'm a member of the weaker sex, I've got news for you: There is no weaker sex!

Biology isn't destiny anymore. Stop patronizing me just because I'm a woman and you think your role in life is to be Mr. Powerful.

I am not any weaker than you. I have personal strength. I have inner strength. I can stand up to a lot more than you think I can. Maybe all this started out as simple politeness, but now it's emerging into an attitude: that I can't do something just because I'm a woman.

I can do *anything* I set my mind to doing, and whether I'm a woman or a man doesn't enter into it. It's because I'm me!

It makes me angry when you take the view that I'm a lesser person than you who couldn't get along without the help of a man.

Take my word for it, I *can*.

And if I have to, I'll prove it.

You don't talk *with* me, you talk *at* me.

We don't have conversations around here. We have lectures. You stand up and pontificate. When I try to respond, you cut me off in mid-sentence and pontificate some more. And you seem to believe that we have a genuine exchange of ideas.

It doesn't work that way.

If you want to have a discussion, you have to give me a chance to speak. You have to listen to what I have to say. You have to remember that it may have some real value. You have to keep an open mind rather than make every decision in your own head and then try to force it down my throat.

I wish you could hear yourself talk. You sound like a preacher in a pulpit trying to place the fear of God's wrath in his congregation. Except in this case, you're not a preacher, the only congregation is me, and God hasn't given you the power of His wrath to evoke.

(Excuse me, *Her* wrath.)

If you want to talk about something as one equal to another, fine. That's all I ask. Just don't hand me this power trip, okay?

Amen.

You don't need a wife or lover. You need a valet.

You're sitting in your favorite chair reading the paper and you say, "Do we have any orange juice?"

What are you, paralyzed? Get your own juice!

Or you're looking in the closet and I hear, "Honey, do I have any clean shirts?" And I think, "What is the story with that man? Is he blind?"

Or you're on your way out the door and I suddenly hear my favorite clarion call: "Say, do you have my keys?"

Grrrr.

I don't have your keys. If you want to know if you have clean shirts, look. There isn't a secret place in this house where we store clean shirts in case of a clean-shirt famine. If you want to know if there's juice or anything else in the fridge, do something radical: Get up, go to the fridge, yank open the door, and *look*!

I'm not here to wait on you hand and foot. You're a fully functional human being. Help yourself.

I hate it when you treat me like a child.

Some women look for men who will be "like a father" to them.

I even know some women in my mother's generation who call their husbands "Daddy" even though they don't have any children.

Maybe it's part of the male role in our society to be paternal. But it's not what I want from you.

I'm not a little girl in a pinafore with a lollypop and braids. I don't need the guiding hand of a father figure. I think my own dad did a pretty good job of bringing me up to be a woman who knows herself, is happy with who she is, and can function confidently, independently, and effectively in the adult world.

I don't need a daddy anymore.

So when you pinch me on the cheek, or tell me to do something because it's good for me, although I know you're being affectionate, you also convey a sense that I'm the little girl in this relationship. If I treated you the way you treat me, in no time we'd be like two kids in a sandbox, fighting over a shovel, waiting for mommy and daddy to step in and referee.

If you disagree with me about this or anything else, remember that I'm too old to be spanked and sent to my room. I'm responsible for myself and by virtue of my participation in this relationship, I'm responsible for you, too.

Doesn't that make me an adult?

INDEX